The Reality
of School
Leadership

Other titles available from Bloomsbury Education:

Achievement for All by Sonia Blandford and Catherine Knowles
The A-Z of School Improvement by Tim Brighouse and David Woods
Creative Educational Leadership by Jacquie Turnbull
The Literacy Leader's Toolkit by Graham Tyrer and Patrick Taylor

The Reality
of School
Leadership

*Coping with the challenges,
reaping the rewards*

Richard Parker
with David Middlewood

B L O O M S B U R Y
LONDON • NEW DELHI • NEW YORK • SYDNEY

Published 2013 by Bloomsbury Education
Bloomsbury Publishing plc
50 Bedford Square, London, WC1B 3DP

www.bloomsbury.com

978-1-4411-9079-6

A CIP record for this publication is available from the British Library.

1 3 5 7 9 10 8 6 4 2

Typeset by Fakenham Prepress Solutions, Fakenham, Norfolk, NR21 8NN
Printed by CPI Group (UK) Ltd, Croydon, CR0 4YY

This book is produced using paper that is made from wood grown in
managed, sustainable forests. It is natural, renewable and recyclable.
The logging and manufacturing processes conform to the environmental
regulations of the country of origin.

Contents

About the authors

Richard Parker spent over 40 years in teaching, nearly half of those in headship. After working in schools in Surrey and Kent, he was appointed to the headship of a technology college in Corby where he stayed for ten years. In 2003 he was appointed to the post of Principal of The Beauchamp College, one of the largest multicultural comprehensives in the country and a school which enjoys a regional, national and international reputation for excellent and innovative practice. In May 2011 it was rated 'outstanding' by Ofsted.

Richard has been heavily involved in professional development programmes throughout his headship and was co-architect in 2000 of the Foundation and Bachelors' degree in Teaching and Learning which now has over 1000 graduates. Both his schools championed the school based masters' programmes set up by the University of Leicester and he himself gained his MBA degree through this route in 1997.

Richard was an associate tutor with the University of Leicester for seven years teaching on the MBA course in educational leadership. He has been a research associate with the (then) National College for School Leadership, a member of the team at the Institute of Education, University of Warwick commissioned to review headteacher succession planning and was, for three years, a council member of the Specialist Schools and Academies Trust.

David Middlewood is a research fellow at the Institute of Education, University of Warwick, having previously worked at the universities of Leicester and Lincoln. This career in Higher Education followed his working in schools for many years , including nine years as a headteacher. David has authored and edited more than 17 books, including ones on strategic management, curriculum management and practitioner research. He is a visiting professor in South Africa and New Zealand, and has been involved in research projects on leadership teams, support staff, inclusive schools, school partnerships and primary school specialisms.

David and Richard have worked together on several occasions and co-authored three previous books on learning schools, extended schools and the research-engaged school. They also co-edited *Headship Matters*, a journal for headteachers for over six years.

Preface

This is a book that I have wanted to write for some time, not just to unravel and rationalise my own thoughts about school leadership but also to seek the opinions of experienced and effective headteachers in the primary and secondary sectors of the UK school system, many of which have been encapsulated in the 'Talking heads' sections that make up parts of Chapters 2 to 9.

Writing the book has also given me the opportunity to see if I could begin to separate the reality from the rhetoric of what is such a complex role. I have frequently discussed the possible approach and content of such a book with friend and co-author David Middlewood but wondered whether I would ever find a publisher willing to allow me to present a very personal take on what, for me, makes headship the best and most enjoyable job in the world.

I say this because from the outset I did not want this to be another research-based book on leadership. The text is deliberately quite lightly referenced and concentrates much more on the practical and pragmatic experience that comes from doing the job day after day. This is no way meant to denigrate the many excellent publications that have emerged on school leadership over the last 30 years but I wanted the freedom to place on record what I, along with several experienced headteachers, believe the real challenges and demands to be. As a result, the book centres on my (still developing!) thoughts and perceptions on how and why the challenges of school leadership are so diverse, so demanding and, if you get it right, so rewarding and fulfilling.

What this book is about

Chapter 1, which David has written, examines what makes school leadership so different from other leadership roles while at the same time drawing attention to the generic skills that sit at the heart of any leadership role.

Chapters 2 and 3 consider the approaches and strategies for securing the top job, the factors determining why some people secure headships and others do not and the early challenges, rewards and demands of taking on the role.

Chapter 4 explores the impact of life history on leadership style and reinforces the need and importance of developing a leadership style that works for you. At the heart of the chapter is the mantra that who and what you are is a product of what has happened in your life. In short, you must maintain the personal integrity that will inevitably define and refine your leadership style.

Chapters 5 to 8 cover the core duties of headship, in particular the need to keep the staff and students motivated, how to find strategies that enable you as a school leader to keep abreast of developments and avoid information overload and, just as important, how to find the right balance when it comes to being in and out of school. Other crucial areas include working with governors, handling the media and establishing effective working links with the local and wider community.

Chapter 9 explores the somewhat neglected challenge of moving on from headship, either to take on new responsibilities or to manage the sometimes difficult transition into retirement. Chapter 10 allows David and me the opportunity to reflect on the issues raised in the book and present some final thoughts on the reality of school leadership.

I cannot over-emphasise how much this is *not* a 'how to be a successful headteacher' handbook and no one contributing to the text, least of all me, is making the claim to have discovered the one truly effective way of taking on what is such a complex and challenging role. Rather, it is a book that presents some educational philosophies, discusses a range of opinions on what makes for effective school leadership and suggests strategies for dealing with the many and various demands placed on heads. It is intended to encourage reflection, disagreement as well as honest and, on occasions, heated debate.

The 'Talking heads' features that run through Chapters 2 to 9 are extracts from the conversations I have had with headteachers over the past two years as part of the research for this book. Like the 'Pause for Thought' boxes, they are intended to provoke reflection and discussion.

The title of the book includes the word 'coping' and this is quite deliberate on the authors' part. The role of headteacher requires a very wide range of often quite different skills, as well as a seemingly encyclopaedic grasp of vast amounts of information and there is no doubt that the pressures can be intense. All of the headteachers interviewed for the book mentioned the unrelenting and, on occasions, quite unreasonable demands of the role and warned of the very real possibility of sinking under the combined weight of the pressures and expectations. It is, therefore, vitally important to have coping strategies in place in order to keep your head above water and maintain a healthy, manageable perspective about how much you can do yourself. In this regard, the experiences and suggestions from seasoned and successful school leaders will, it is hoped, provide some food for thought.

As soon as you set about writing a book like this, you realise that the more solutions you present, the more problems and questions appear. I have already said that there is no 'quick fix' to ensure successful school leadership and all the books in the world will not adequately prepare anyone who is considering taking on the role, because, as one of the interviewees observed, the best preparation for headship is headship itself. However, I hope that what is offered here is an opportunity for you to listen to my views, to David's views and the opinions of people who, for whatever reason, have taken on headship and survived and prospered in the role.

Acknowledgements

This book would not have happened without David Middlewood. As I have said, he has spent countless hours with me over the last few years discussing the possible content and practicality of writing a book on the reality of school leadership like this and has been unfailingly supportive in helping me take my early ideas and turn them into words. As a highly experienced and well regarded author who has already co-authored three books with me, he has also brought his considerable and invaluable expertise and knowledge to help me edit and refine the text as well as contributing the opening chapter and co-writing Chapter 10. I am in his debt and cannot thank him enough for his constant support and encouragement.

Of course, the people who have contributed more than anyone else to the writing of this book have been the countless young people and adults I have worked with during my teaching career. I must pay tribute as well to the many primary and secondary school heads who willingly gave up so much of their precious time to be interviewed for the book. There is absolutely no doubt that their collected wisdom has made a vital contribution and without their views and insights any opinions offered by David and/or me would, as a consequence, have been so much the poorer.

Thanks are also due to my wife Nora who, as a fellow headteacher, has been a very perceptive and well-informed sounding board who made sure that I kept to editorial deadlines. I would also like to thank my son Stephen for his advice and suggestions for improving the text and to my other sons, Christopher and Jonny, for their constant support of and interest in my work as a headteacher.

Thanks also to Pam Morey for her help in preparing the proofs for publication.

Finally, many thanks to Bloomsbury for their support and advice and for allowing me the opportunity to consider, rationalise, define and finally put into words why I loved the reality of being a headteacher as much as I did.

Richard Parker
May 2013

1 Why is school leadership unique?

Chapter overview

This opening chapter sets the scene by exploring what it is really like to be a headteacher or principal of a school. It considers the uniqueness of school leadership primarily by:

- Discussing the importance of leadership, and what leadership is.
- Exploring the differences between leadership and management.
- Examining leadership activities and skills that are common across a number of different fields.
- Comparing leadership in the public and private sectors.
- Discussing the differences between educational leadership and leadership in other fields.
- Suggesting some ways in which school leadership is unique.

As authors of this book we strongly believe that school leadership *is* unique and that although it has some things in common with other kinds of leadership, there is nothing quite like leading a school. In this first chapter, I have tried to put school leadership in context through the sections listed above, showing *why* it is unique, and the following chapters by Richard Parker illustrate graphically *how* it is so.

Leadership: its importance and interpretation

There is a plethora of literature on leadership; indeed it has been described as an industry in itself. Any scrutiny of the bookshelves of a bookshop or of a relevant website shows books on leadership written by those in business, industry, politics, public services and by various consultants and 'self-help' gurus. We are told that good leadership is vital for success in almost every field of activity, so that captains of national sporting teams, notably cricket and rugby union in the UK, have written bestsellers on the subject too. It is a topic of enormous importance to many people not least because it appears to offer career opportunities, which they believe will be denied to them if they cannot show that they possess the necessary qualities and potential.

Leadership in education is similarly widely written about, although rarely found in the bestsellers' lists. It is taught up to higher degree level in virtually all universities in developed countries. Academic journals are focused on it, just as numerous conferences and programmes are devoted to the development of leadership skills and understanding. It is worth considering therefore what leadership is, or is claimed or believed to be, in order to understand its importance today.

What is leadership?

Definitions of leadership abound and later in this chapter what may make it distinct from management, administration and other related terms is debated. However, if we start with what can generally be agreed upon, we can say that leadership:

- is vitally important to the success of any organisation
- comes in many different forms
- shows itself in various different ways
- does not restrict itself to one type of person who defines outstanding leadership
- is intentional in that it sets out to achieve something.

The nature of leadership means that it inevitably involves the influence of a person or persons over other people 'to structure the activities and relationships in a group or organisation' (Yukl, 2002). However, while influence can be exerted by anyone, leadership tends to have both influence *and* authority linked in its execution, sometimes, although not necessarily always, involving a formal position in an organisation.

It is possible to identify some crucial things that leadership involves:

- setting the vision for an organisation
- developing strategies to achieve that vision
- influencing and developing an appropriate organisational culture
- ensuring accountability to stakeholders
- motivating and developing the workforce
- ensuring sustainability.

This list will be returned to later in the chapter, but of course leadership per se is an abstract concept and manifests itself through the actions and behaviour of those acting as leaders. In other words, leadership is only real when we see it, hear it, respond to it, read it, or note the results of it in action. After 11 September 2001 ('9/11') the Mayor of New York, Rudy Guliani, wrote about leaders: 'Most of your ability to get people to do what they have to do is going to depend on what they perceive when they look at you and listen to you. They need to see someone who is stronger than they are, but human too'. Harris (2005) said that the reality of leadership lies in 'individual connection and personal compassion'. Other people need to see something in the leader that they can connect with and about which they have feelings. Stoll and Fink (1996) argued for 'invitational leadership' whereby others, individually and in groups, were invited to participate in leadership activities; this process developed into a culture of sharing and thereby helping to build a shared vision.

Fink (2005) suggests that the qualities a leader needs to possess in order for others to wish to accept the invitations include:

- reason
- memory
- imagination
- intuition
- common sense
- ethics.

It is hard to disagree with this list, and more could be added of course, but two of them are worth reflecting on here in the context of the experiences of various leaders described in later chapters of this book.

Common sense and intuition

These two qualities may not be as different from each other in action as might be supposed. For leaders, they are often used in situations where, for example, a decision has to be taken on the spur of the moment, when there is no time to gather data. Similarly, when there seems to be several options or when evidence appears to be contradictory, the leader has to be able to say, 'We'll do this', or 'We'll go for that one'. In reality, the line between common sense and gut instinct is a very thin one.

Each of these qualities, as with all others, has its drawbacks if overused. Too much reliance on intuition could lead to prejudice and create uncertainty among those relying on the leadership. Using common sense all the time can stifle any sense of excitement and innovation. Underpinning the application of any or all of the qualities possessed by an effective leader is surely a clear set of values. These values, developed through upbringing and life experience, provide the basis for any leadership philosophy and therefore for leadership behaviour. Understanding the importance of values links with the issue of emotions in leaders. The crucial relevance of emotional intelligence, developed by Daniel Goleman in the 1990s, has enabled many to realise that a leader's ability to develop meaningful relationships with others and help others to develop themselves relies heavily on the emotional context established by that leader.

Much of this raises the familiar question as to whether leadership can be taught, or even whether leaders are 'born or made' (see Chapter 4). There is no doubt that particular skills helpful in effective leadership operations can be learnt, but there remains significant debate as to the extent to which many of the things inherent in successful leadership can really be acquired through training courses, conferences or leadership programmes. Leadership is surely an art or, as Grint (2003) called it, 'an array of arts'. If leadership is art, is management science? This chapter now considers these two fields so closely linked when it comes to the leadership of organisations.

Is leadership really different from management?

Ideas change over time and the context within which ideas flourish also change. General management theory was initially rational and 'scientific' with the emphasis being on processes such as organising, co-ordinating, planning and problem-solving (Fayol, 1916). The focus here was on control and being able to direct in some way.

'A manager therefore was someone [who was] sorting out the problems that cannot be dealt with in the normal arrangements of day-to-day activities'. (Crawford, 2003)

In schools, this understanding led to the arrival of the person who was the manager of all the teaching of a subject in a secondary school – the 'Head of the Department' and the manger of the pastoral welfare of a year cohort of students – the 'Head of Year'. Although there was a clear divide between what were regarded as 'academic' and 'pastoral' matters (much less blurred than it is in today's schools) these people, previously known as the 'Senior English Master' or 'Senior Maths Mistress', in the main assumed managerial tasks primarily relating to resources. The emergence of more posts at the head of the school's hierarchy, especially second or third deputy heads in large schools, led to the development in the late 1960s and 1970s of the Senior Management Team.

Traditional leadership theories basically focused on management techniques; the skills involved in managing, and applying these to the set goals of an organisation in order for them to be achieved. Later, certainly since the late 1970s, leadership came to be seen as more transformational, helping to shape the views of members of the organisation and proposing ideas for the future. The influence of leaders on such notions as vision or culture began to be seen as important, while a manager was seen as more transactional in helping to achieve the agreed goals. The famous aphorism of Warren Bennis summed up the perceived distinction between leaders and managers: 'managers do things right; leaders do the right things'.

Leadership vs management?

But in the twenty-first century, how different are leadership and management? Is it really just a matter of semantics and a debate that does not illuminate what really matters, namely what is achieved? This book is entitled *The Reality of School Leadership*. In 1989, Torrington and Weightman wrote a book called *The Reality of School Management* and it looked at how schools operated. This is a useful indicator of the changing of ideas and language in education. In 1990, when the UK government set up a group to investigate the running of schools, it was called the School Management Task Force; in 1997, a national institution for training and developing headteachers was called the National College for School Leadership. In 2005, Hoyle and Wallace noted that only fairly recently had 'leadership' taken over from 'management' as the main way of describing operating and improving public institutions.

Cuban (1988) made a distinction between leadership and management in seeing the former as about change and the latter as about maintenance: 'By leadership, I mean influencing others' actions in achieving desirable ends... Managing is maintaining efficiently and effectively current organisational arrangements'.

Leadership is increasingly linked with values and also with vision and mission. However, as Fullan (1992) reminds us, building a vision is a highly sophisticated and dynamic process, which is difficult for most organisations to sustain.

Ultimately, effective leadership and effective management are equally essential if organisations are to achieve their goals. Cuban (1988), quoted above on the distinction between them, made it clear that he prized both and attached no prioritising value to either one because different times and settings needed varied responses. A failing organisation may be failing because it is poorly managed and the top priority for any new person taking charge may well be to put efficient and effective management processes in place to save it from extinction, before paying attention to a long-term vision for its future. We know too of many leaders who had plenty of vision but lacked the necessary skills to turn that vision into reality.

Bolman and Deal (1997, p.xxii) also stressed that both leadership and management are important: 'The challenge of modern organisations requires the objective perspective of the manager as well as the flashes of vision and commitment wise leadership provides'. This quote, however, does seem to imply that leaders are in some way superior to managers (more intuitive, more emotional, more exciting perhaps), something that many do not agree with. Some see management as an overall term that embraces leadership, while Crawford (2003) sees what is commonly called leadership as 'highly effective intuitive management'. She makes the point that if we exalt leadership to too lofty levels, making it seem exceptional, then few people may feel they can aspire to be leaders. She sees 'inventive management and wise leadership' as complementary functions, both essential to successful organisations.

Other terms impinge on this debate. In North America and Australia, for example, the term 'administration' is widely used to describe the work of those seen as leaders or managers in the UK, where 'administration' generally refers to 'paperwork' or 'office work'; a school administrator in the UK is likely to be a bursar or secretary, but an overall 'leader' in a US college. West-Burnham, at a seminar in 1994, described leadership as 'path-finding', management as 'path-following', and administration as 'path-tidying'. Similarly,

Covey (1994) described managers as those who follow the workers who are cutting their way through the jungle, clearing the undergrowth. They prepare development programmes and work out schedules. The leader is 'the one who climbs the tallest tree, surveys the entire situation, and yells, 'Wrong jungle!' (Covey, 1994, p.101)

One other term, 'managerialism', is commonly given a negative connotation, meaning 'managing to excess' (Bush et al., 2010, p.4) or managing minutiae. Managerialism can result from losing sight of essential purpose ('Why are we doing this?') and it is this focus on purposes, along with the values that underpin them which defines leadership – and management – as of prime importance in taking organisations forward.

So does it matter, this distinction between leadership and management, if indeed there is one? What is certain is that effectiveness in both is essential for any organisation to succeed, that good leaders need also to be good managers and that the job of a leader will involve both leadership and management and, it must be said, some administration as well!

Pause for thought

- Think about what leadership means to you and what type of leader you think best suits your strengths and aspirations.
- Consider the differences between common sense and intuition. How much would you look to one or both of these tools to help you lead an organisation effectively?
- Try to understand the place and importance of leadership and management in a school leader's role. Acknowledge the extent to which they are complementary rather than conflicting skills – if used wisely!

Leadership factors common in most fields of activity

With literally thousands of texts written about the elements of successful leadership and management in many different spheres of human activity, it would be presumptuous to attempt anything more than a brief summary here of what these can include, and therefore the focus is on the list from page 3.

Setting the vision for an organisation

Without a vision of what an organisation aims to be, it can lose its way and suffer from a sense of purposelessness. This vision needs to be challenging and ambitious, but also rooted in reality. Reality here may include the environment within which the organisation operates, the market, and the regulations governing its operation. Within these limits, vision is perhaps *the* key element in successful leadership. Of course, trends and fashions come and go in this field as elsewhere and there are periods of scepticism about the actual word 'vision.' This is neatly encapsulated in the anecdote of the US principal in the 1990s who supposedly said, 'In my early days, if I'd said I'd got a vision, the men in white coats would have been called; now you can't get a job without one!'

Sometimes, leaders attempt to condense the expression of the vision into a mission statement, another term whose favour waxes and wanes. How many of us for instance can quote the mission statement of our own organisation?

Developing strategies to achieve that vision

A vision becomes pointless unless there are clear ideas about how it can be achieved, and the leader's ability to think strategically and help others to do so is crucial. 'If you don't know where you are going, anywhere will do' was a saying from the Koran often quoted by one school leader (Parker, 1997). Strategic thinking and developing a strategic plan is of a higher order than is required at an everyday or operational level. The differences are shown in simple form in the table on the next page.

Influencing and developing an appropriate organisational culture

This is one of the topics most commonly written about by leaders in business and industry – how the inculcating of a set of values and beliefs in all employees can lead to successful performance. Whether these values are, for example, 'quality first, all the time' or 'client service comes above everything else' or 'value for money'.

These beliefs can sit at the heart of successful businesses as long as they are enacted. Most of us in our roles in society as retail customers or clients recognise an organisation, whether retail, restaurant, entertainment or service, where we will return again and again because of our confidence that certain values are being practised all the time, even when mistakes occur.

Differences between strategic and operational thinking

Strategic thinking is...	Operational thinking is...
Longer term	Short term, immediate
In whole organisational terms	About the area needing attention
Reflective	Leading to quick action
Idealistic, 'visionary'	Practical, pragmatic
Conceptual	Concrete
About using whole organisational capabilities	About using accessible resources
Breaking new ground	Ongoing, routine
About effectiveness	About efficiency
Identifying opportunities	Resolving current problems
Examining the external context	Focusing on internal context
A 'hands-off' approach	A 'hands-on' approach
With a 'helicopter' perspective	With a 'down to earth' perspective

Middlewood (1998, p.8)

Ensuring accountability to stakeholders

In business organisations, this accountability is ultimately to the customers or clients, the board of management and the shareholders. The leader's role is to establish and develop a structure of accountability for all those in the organisation, but knowing all the while that the ultimate accountability for the performance is his or hers. It is this feature that has prompted various leaders to comment on the isolation and loneliness of those individuals at the top. It is also the one that brings perhaps the greatest stress and challenges but also the most excitement.

Motivating and developing the workforce

This is closely linked with the organisational culture of course, but also involves the commitment to ongoing training, enabling research into training requirements, job satisfaction of employees, and all the many factors which contribute to employees wanting to work there. Being fulfilled in their work and having opportunities to progress and develop both as an individual and as a member of the organisation are crucial to motivation. Again, appropriate structures will be in place but the literature on successful business organisations suggests that employees in them have an admiration for their overall leader and his or her style, even when they have never personally met them because of the sheer size of the company.

Ensuring sustainability

No organisation can succeed in the twenty-first century without leadership which is concerned with sustainability. In a world with many ephemeral aspects (the 'quick fix', the 'use it and throw away' elements), the need for an organisation to demonstrate its clear commitment to the future as well as the present, to the wider community as well as its own narrow segment of it, to the environment in all its forms (physical, social, moral), is paramount.

Each of the above aspects offers scope for a debate in itself. The purpose here has simply been to indicate that leadership, wherever it exists, has some things in common. Before considering how leadership in education may differ from that in other contexts, it is worth reflecting on what differences may affect the operation of leadership in two separate spheres; private enterprise and public or state ownership.

Leadership in the public and private sectors

Education is a 'state business' in many countries, like health, transport, law and order but it should be noted that in many developing countries parents are still expected to pay fees towards the cost of schooling. In those developed countries where resource-based management exists and some form of delegated responsibility is given to individual schools or colleges, there is a greater move towards more of a 'free market' in educational provision, involving competition between institutions. Of course, this can never be more than a 'quasi-market' because schools and colleges are guaranteed their basic clients (learners) through the state's need to provide education as a right. We can reflect briefly on some of the basic differences between the public and private sectors and the implications of these differences for the leadership at operational level in institutions.

1 The public sector organisation is guaranteed to exist, whereas the private sector one has no 'right to exist'. (Of course individual schools close and new ones open, but schools per se continue to exist.)

2 The public sector organisation has a guaranteed income from national government; the private sector one must 'win' this income.

3 The public sector must implement changes according to legislation, although schools will do this in different ways; the private sector will initiate change to gain new customers and improve profit, for example. 'Continuous improvement' is more theoretical in public services; private sector organisations are driven by need, and constantly have to seek new ways of doing things.

4 Public sector organisations are more inwardly focused; private sector ones are constantly looking at competitors and striving to win contracts against those competitors, with huge implications for the costs involved.

5 Public sector organisations, because they have accountability for public money, usually have effective systems for tracking budgets, investment in management information systems, good 'historical' data; private sector ones spend much less time on what is seen as essentially 'non-productive' work.

All of these differences are being blurred in the context of the increasingly autonomous schools, for example, in England and Wales and the US, with new types of schools being given much greater licence to run their own affairs and make decisions that benefit them as individual schools. This blurring is also evident when we realise that, while the above distinctions apply to small and medium sized private firms and businesses, many larger and increasingly globalised corporations, ironically because of their scale, are having to operate more like public service organisations in terms of accountability systems, for example.

The implications of these differences for leadership at individual institutional level (although increasingly blurred) are perhaps mainly in terms of the way personnel are led and managed. Leaders in education and other sectors have to be much more aware of human rights legislation which can lead to a wariness about employment tribunals and judicial reviews. Education in many countries has battled with the issue, for example, of how to dismiss under-performing teachers; the response to poor performance in the private sector can be swifter and more ruthless. A charity business that provides for vulnerable adults, for example, cannot tolerate weak performance where that adult is at risk, whereas a school can often struggle to remove a weak teacher despite the vulnerability of the children in his/her care.

In terms of pay, public sector leaders must normally pay staff within nationally laid down agreed rates (although this is becoming significantly less rigid with the increase of much more autonomous schools), while private firms can set their own rates, taking account of the market for such staff as they require. Again, the trend in the new types of schools mentioned above (for example, academies in England and Wales) is to give leaders the scope to pay at their own special rates and award bonuses for good performance.

Middle leaders or managers in private sector organisations tend to have much greater autonomy in decision-making and have to 'live or die' by these decisions; although autonomy for middle leaders is increasing significantly in educational institutions, a poor decision is unlikely to cost the post holder their job.

Another significant area of difference between public and private sectors is that of recruitment and selection of leaders. For example, and this is very relevant to Chapters 2 and 3 in this book which describe the UK experience, the system in the countries of the UK is markedly different from that in many other developed countries. It is a 'lottery', depending on potential applicants surveying the market and applying for whichever and however many jobs they wish, until they succeed in being selected and appointed by the governors of a particular school. From that point, the new leader remains there (barring accident, forcible removal or scandal) until they decide to apply for another post – or decide to retire. This is the same system that is used throughout the educational system, from beginning teachers, through mid-career promotion, right through to applying for inspectorate posts.

In other countries such as Japan, several states of Australia, Canada, the US and many European countries, the system can be very different. Although it varies from country to country or state to state, candidates for principalship are assessed by the appropriate body, according to prescribed criteria, and then deemed suitable (or not) for the post of principal. Depending on the precise system, they can then put their names forward (or their names can be put forward by a third party) for a school within the region for which they have been approved, or they are allocated to a school by the approving authority. The post is usually for a fixed-term period, typically five to seven years. At the end of that period, principals can be re-allocated to a different school, a larger one, for example. In some systems this stage and the proposed new school is negotiable.

Each system clearly has its merits and demerits; the purpose here is not to assess these (for a full discussion, see Middlewood, 2010: 133–6), but to point out the differences. The particular challenge for countries and states where there is a strong movement towards even greater autonomy for schools (for example, charter schools in the US and academies and free schools in England) is how to reconcile this increasing decentralisation with a need to ensure a supply of highly-effective leaders for those schools that are least popular and which inevitably emerge in what is in effect a free market in education.

None of the above differences can guarantee in themselves successful and effective leadership. It is clear that there are as many effective and ineffective leaders in both the public and the private sectors, the brilliant and the banal exist in both areas. It could easily be argued that an outstanding leader in a public sector institution deserves even more of an accolade than a private sector counterpart but in reality the debate is ultimately futile because of the different needs and cultures. Certainly, education, rightly or wrongly, is constantly being exhorted by politicians to learn from so-called 'best practice' in the private sector. This stance is partly driven by 'political imperatives, satisfying the ideologically driven view that the private sector has much to teach, and little to learn from education.' (Bell and Bush, 2002, p.6)

However, 'best practice' is rarely defined and such exhortations fail to take account of the significant differences discussed above, and more importantly perhaps, the special nature of education as an inalienable human right. Seldom do politicians expect business to learn from education!

Differences between leadership in education and in other contexts

Initial interest in using management processes in schools, colleges and universities consisted simply of applying business or industrial models to them. As educational management – later leadership – developed into a discipline in its own right, worthy for example of its own literature, study and research, attention often focused on those aspects 'special' to education. Although, as discussed earlier, leadership has many elements common across all spheres of activity, it is worth considering the features of educational organisations which make them different from most others, and therefore affect the kind of leadership necessary for effectiveness.

West-Burnham (1992) and Bush (1996) suggested some of these differences and, drawing upon their work and adding others, the following list is proposed. Some of the features are of course found in certain other non-commercial organisations, but the list as a whole is relevant to education specifically.

The objectives of educational organisations are less clear cut

In commercial organisations, issues of profit, material products or outcomes can be carefully delineated. Although some may consider it easy to define the objective of a good school, for example, these definitions are usually expressed in terms such as 'provide a good, all-round education', words, on scrutiny, that are vague. What is 'good'? What is 'all-round'? What is 'education' in this context? Governments and politicians are fond of suggesting that the whole thing is really very simple at heart but it manifestly is not.

Currently, in many developed countries, there is intense debate about how to reconcile the achieving of one set of objectives, namely gaining an appropriate number of qualifications, certificates and the like with the other objective of preparing young people for employability through providing them with skills such as communication, co-operation and team working. Begley (2010) suggests three dimensions to the educational process, namely:

- the aesthetic (involving for example self-esteem, personal fulfilment, lifelong learning)
- the economic (involving preparation for a career, developing relevant skills for employability)
- the socialisation (involving citizenship in its broadest sense, social skills).

It is easy to see that different stakeholders in education perceive the main objectives of schools and colleges to be allied to their own interests. For example, it could be argued that educational professionals traditionally saw aesthetic purposes as the primary purpose, while many employers and parents see the economic as the most important purpose. A report on the riots of the summer 2011 which broke out in a number of British cities focused partly on the socialisation aspects of education as being fundamental to avoiding future occurrences of such disturbances, including blaming 'poor parenting'; however, it also suggested that schools might actually be fined when basic literacy standards were not achieved for individuals as this contributed to lack of employment for many youths.

The measurement of outcomes of the educational process is very difficult

Given the ambiguity of objectives, it is not surprising that measuring them is difficult. At government level, international comparisons primarily focus on the measurement of attainment through test and examination results. Only a minor emphasis is given in these comparisons to outcomes relating to, for example, citizenship or social skills. Since each of the three purposes noted on the previous page involves basically a different kind of learning;

- aesthetic = transformational
- economic = transactional
- socialisation = transmissional

the capacity to measure the outcomes of a school or college in precise terms is necessarily extremely limited.

There is an ambiguity about who is the clientele

Unlike many other organisations, defining the clientele for schools and colleges is not straightforward. For teachers, the child or student is clearly their client on a daily basis but they may feel that the parents are really the persons to whom they are responsible in terms of what they achieve for their children.

The lines of accountability are blurred

Bush (1996) uses the word 'fragmented' to describe the organisation and structure 'which impinges upon educational institutions'. (Bush, 1996, p.9) A plethora of external agencies and others impact on the working of a school or college. These include:

- governors
- community groups
- parental groups
- inspection and advisory services
- local and national politicians
- local employers
- sponsors
- regional authorities.

There is no clear-cut equivalent to a commercial company's shareholders, despite the fact that in England and Wales the introduction of a Parents' Annual General

Meeting was advocated by the then Secretary of State for Education as being equivalent to an annual report to shareholders.

Children are at the centre of the process

Having children or young people at the centre of the process in education makes it very different from dealing with the raw materials of an industry or commercial business. Mandatory education is sometimes referred to as the 'one chance only' process for those involved. Children are in compulsory education for about ten years in most developed countries. They cannot be experimented upon in trials in laboratories; they cannot be thrown away if the process fails on a 'let's try again' basis. If there is a raw material, it is the hearts and minds of children and young people, factors that cannot be programmed or processed in any formulaic way.

Also, given the large amount of time a pupil or student spends with specific teachers over a period of years, the importance of relationships becomes central to effective teaching and learning, and this is clearly an area with potential for inconsistency and even contradiction. A further point of interest is the current growth in the notion of 'student voice.' The fact that the actual recipients of the educational process are being increasingly encouraged to offer views on the service they receive is an additional strong indication of the differences between educational and most other organisations. This is a quite separate thing from the voice of employees where teachers and other staff can be seen as similar to other employees in that respect. The nearest equivalent to student voice is perhaps that of the 'patient voice' gradually developing in various health services.

The professional composition of the workforce

Although the importance of support staff in schools and college has increased significantly and the need to lead and manage the whole workforce is crucial (see Bush and Middlewood, 2013), it is still true that these places are predominantly staffed by people with a common professional background. The teachers share the same initial training and professional background as their leaders and managers. The key element in any kind of professionalism is a degree of autonomy, which is epitomised in the essentially solitary nature of classroom teaching, i.e. one professional adult in a room with a number of children or young persons, a situation which occurs from the first day of entry into the profession. This professional feature of the workforce, while not unique to education, is hugely significant for the way in which decisions are reached and policies implemented.

The background and experience of educational leaders

Unlike many leaders in business and industry, leadership in educational institutions is carried out by people whose careers involved teaching or lecturing. Often, they have had little intention of becoming headteachers or principals and entered the teaching profession simply because they wanted to teach! Gaining experience through leading subject departments or year cohorts of students in primary or secondary schools, or in post-statutory colleges, they progress to middle/senior leadership positions and finally to school or college leadership.

Progression from that post is likely to take them to another leadership post, perhaps of a larger establishment, or to an inspection or advisory role at regional or national level within the education sector. At present, it is very rare for anyone to become the leader of a school without previously having had a career, however short or long, in teaching. Indeed, it is still the case in some countries that lengthy experience in teaching is virtually the *only* criterion for headship. In many European countries (Watson, 2003) and in most of Africa (Bush and Odura, 2006) it is the fact that the only qualification for headship of schools is experience in teaching (see Bush, 2008). The specific preparation of people for school leadership is still a comparatively recent initiative, reflecting more than anything else the extent to which the role has grown in complexity and accountability over the last 20 years.

A successful executive leader in one sphere of business can sometimes be transferred or gain a post in a different sphere, especially in the public sector in the belief that the skills and abilities which have proved effective in one context can readily be effectively used in another. This does not happen in education, although as schools and colleges increasingly become 'businesses' in this century, it is a topic that is occasionally mooted. The model of an executive principal at the head of a group of schools, each with its own individual leader, already exists and may be moving the system towards the time when such personnel are not seen as being required to have an educational background.

The very rare occurrence to date of a person with no teaching experience being appointed to a headship illustrates the fact that governments and school governors are extremely wary about taking such a bold step. The fact that the people who have been appointed through this route have been spectacularly unsuccessful in the role would seem to justify the degree of caution being shown. Of course, there is at the present time no concrete proof as to whether the reason for the failure was the calibre of the candidate, the uniqueness of school leadership or the lack of any teaching experience.

The special nature of school leadership

In the above section, a number of features have been suggested which make educational organisations different from most other kinds and therefore affect the kind of leadership necessary for effectiveness. Finally in this chapter, it is necessary to try to identify some further aspects which are specific to schools themselves, so that school leadership can be envisioned in the context of the chapters that follow in this book.

Compared with universities, polytechnics, colleges of further education and similar post-statutory education institutions, there are four factual features of schools which have an impact on the way they are led and managed, namely:

- their size
- the ages of their learners
- the fact that attendance is mandatory
- the fact there is little time allowed for leadership activity.

Different systems operate in different countries but, broadly speaking, education systems are structured in three phases: primary, secondary and tertiary. Although a small number of 'all-through' schools exist, (for example, three to 18, four to 16 years or five to 18 years) and a number also cross mandatory school age attendance ages (for example, 14 to 18 years), the vast majority of systems operate in these three phases. It is salutary, in noting this, that the United Nations' aim of universal *primary* education is still a long way from being achieved in many developing nations.

The size of schools as organisations

Compared with universities or colleges catering for post-statutory learners, schools are mostly smaller organisations. Universities often have more than 20,000 personnel, post-statutory colleges typically anything between 3,000 and 9,000, including many part-time learners and staff. In the UK, a very small number of secondary schools have around 2,000 students, and a typical one has between 700 and 1,400 students. The range in primary education is far greater. An early years school may have no more than 30 children, primary schools (especially in rural areas) between 40 and 60 pupils, and larger ones up to 900, with a typical size being between 200 and 500. Each one of these has to be led and managed, with the stakeholders of each one demanding effective leadership.

The relative smallness of most schools therefore implies that the leadership and management of them will involve a degree of intimacy with all individual internal clients (learners and staff), which is extremely difficult in many cases and not expected at a university for example. While not expecting that the leader of a secondary or large primary school would be certain to know the name and nature of each individual pupil or student, there is an expectation from parents especially that access to the leader should be made possible through the school's structures and systems.

The ages of the learners

As discussed earlier, having children or young people at the heart of the process has significant implications for the leading of educational organisations. In the case of schools, providing for children as young as three years old to at least 15 or 16 years old, these implications are profound. The fact that the school, all those that work there, and ultimately, the headteacher or principal is 'in loco parentis' is something unique to this sector of education. While teachers and their leaders are not expected to *be* parents – they have specific professional duties and tasks to perform – nevertheless, they have a duty of care, both legal and moral, on behalf of the children and young people in attendance. In legal terms, all educational organisations, indeed all kinds of organisations, have a duty of care to all employees and students in, for example, health and safety, but the responsibilities of schools go much further. Going well beyond minimum legal requirements, the effective leadership and management of schools involves establishing and developing a culture and ethos which is appropriate, perhaps supportive yet challenging within clear parameters, to each individual child or young person.

The fact that attendance is compulsory

This often overlooked aspect of schooling, in terms of its implications for leadership, is one that makes it unique among educational organisations. No other institutions (apart from prisons perhaps!) require its daily personnel to be in attendance because the law requires them to be there. While this attendance is part and parcel of the normality of a country's culture, as much as any other feature of daily life, it makes it 'special' for those that work in schools, compared with post-statutory colleges where the student has chosen to attend.

School leaders face particular challenges during, for example, the period of adolescence when questioning and challenging the status quo are the norm. If we note that puberty reaches children at no one specific age, and each child is unique anyway, the challenge for leaders of schools with those pupils is to maintain the motivation and relevant learning focus for all the students in their care. Moreover, the period of statutory state education tends to be lengthened as countries develop and link the economic prosperity of the nation to the state education provided. In England and Wales, for instance, the school leaving age was raised from 14 years to 15 years in the late 1940s, from 15 to 16 in the early 1970s, and from 16 to 18 in 2013.

There is little time allowed for leadership activity

Unlike their counterparts in business and industry, educational leaders have comparatively little time to carry out duties specific to leadership or management. In many schools, particularly primary schools, the headteacher is expected to continue to teach in the classroom. Generally speaking, the smaller the school, the more time the headteacher is required to teach, so that in a very small primary school, he or she may have as little as half a day a week to focus on leadership or management duties, including paperwork. Even in larger secondary schools, deputy principals may teach for a considerable part of their time and middle leaders will have perhaps the equivalent of between half a day and a day per week for leadership of their departments. This is not to argue that this is undesirable but simply to make the point, as shown below, that time for leadership duties in schools is extremely limited in view of the huge variety of other operational tasks that go hand in hand with the role.

Given that the four features discussed above are ones that are unique to their leadership, what implications do they have for the reality of school leadership? Probably this uniqueness is best shown in any scrutiny of the daily reality of life in a school. Of course, a headteacher, like counterparts elsewhere, has meetings with colleagues or visitors or agencies to debate issues, to recruit and select staff, to propose plans and suggest solutions to problems. But these have to be fitted in alongside the hurly burly of daily life in a busy school, full of children and young people all demanding and expecting attention.

Unlike chief executives, headteachers will have to maintain a clear overview of the organisation's key aims and objectives while at the same time doing lunchtime duties, maybe some teaching, dealing with difficult children, meeting demanding parents and on occasions picking up litter! General managers of national banks are not expected to spend part of every day on the tills – they would never see that as part of their role.

During development programmes over the years for aspiring, newly-appointed and long-serving school leaders (e.g. NPQH, HEADLAMP, NPQSL), many partici-pants have kept journals, diaries or logs of their daily routines at work. What consistently emerges from reading these is an awareness of the astonishing variety of incidents, unexpected tasks, trivial occurrences, emergency problems that they find themselves caught up in, even on an official 'walkabout'. A small sample would include:

- praising a student for work or good manners in opening a door
- admonishing a student for incorrect dress, running dangerously, dropping litter etc.
- gently admonishing a member of staff for being late to a class
- finding a student wandering and dealing with the situation
- listening to a staff problem or being given an update on any particular issue
- making any number of decisions to issues/requests raised by staff in the corridors – extremely carefully and diplomatically!
- noting displays of work – good or bad
- being reminded of paperwork outstanding
- noting a repair that needs to be done
- reacting to invitations to classes, to deal with incidents
- being told about an unexpected visitor
- dealing with an intruder on site.

These diaries give a picture of a daily life which begins at home perhaps with a phone call about a staff problem or concern, includes a visit from a distraught parent, a complaint from a neighbour of the school, a consideration of an idea about fund raising and even noting that the goldfish had to be fed before heading home! Add to these the assemblies, the functions to be supported, the requests for resources and the visits to other local schools, and many other activities, and the extreme multi-tasking nature of the work becomes clear.

Why is there such an extraordinary variety, and a concern for the minutiae of daily life here? In schools, the concern is for both the process (above all of learning) *and* the product (narrowly defined here as an 'outcome', such as being able to read). Of course, leaders and managers in all organisations need to ensure the process is effective so that the outcome is a successful one, but school leaders must focus equally on *both*. Any leader would argue that a satisfied and motivated employee will of course produce a better outcome and that everything that can be done should be done to achieve that motivation and job satisfaction. For school leaders, the task goes beyond that because trying to ensure that motivation and sense of fulfilment in each individual child or young person is an end in itself, as well as enabling them to achieve a successful outcome, such as reaching a good standard in mathematics.

They have to do all this at a time when some young people may be becoming aware that they are only at school because the law says they have to be and may be questioning this, and when they and/or their parents may all be demanding these successful outcomes. It is also the time when human biological development is at one of its fastest stages of change, from early years, through childhood and adolescence to young adulthood. All the 'normal' complications of emotional and physical development, sexual awakening, moral questioning and the complexities of authority and independence are to be catered for, sometimes supported by the child's home but sometimes anything but. Whether it is seen as the most exciting of jobs, or the most impossibly challenging of jobs, it is little wonder that school leaders say that there is no other job like it.

Action points

- Because school leadership *is* special, take time to research the role as carefully and comprehensively as possible.
- Take every opportunity to talk candidly with experienced headteachers or principals to find out how they do the job and how they manage the pressure. Ask them about the highs and lows of the job.
- Never assume that there is only one way of doing the job. Listen to the views of those you respect. You do not have to agree with them all but the range of approaches to leadership will be revealing.
- The job at the top can be a lonely one but the loneliest headteachers are those who do not relate well to people. Leading, managing and getting on with people is an absolutely essential skill for school leaders.

2 Taking control of your career

Chapter overview

This chapter will deal with how you ensure that you keep control of your career up to and including headship. Key areas to explore will include:

- The importance of regular and consistent self assessment.
- Keeping track of short-/mid-/long-term future needs.
- The importance of being proactive and resilient when preparing for headship.
- Accessing the best possible professional development.
- The need to regularly take on new roles and responsibilities.
- How to maintain confidence in your ability to make a difference in whatever role you are doing!
- Making sure you are as marketable as possible.

Keeping tabs on where you are in your career

In Chapter 3 I refer to the fact that there are people who are genuinely interested in developing their careers and there are those who talk a good career but ultimately have little or no real intention of progressing from where they currently are. Many people are comfortable with their particular lot but feel obliged to present a face that appears to be ambitious and disaffected with what they are doing but in reality they are quite settled and do not have any real desire to take on the challenges and stresses of senior leadership. And there is nothing wrong with that.

We all know colleagues who have been in the same school for the whole of their working lives and are entirely comfortable with the status quo. They may have different roles and obtain promotion without ever changing schools and maintain that they are challenged each and every day. I knew from the outset that I could never have stayed in the same school for the whole of my teaching career and although I never worked out where that conviction came from, it stayed with me throughout my working life. Others feel no such pressure – indeed some teachers would consider it an act of betrayal to leave 'their' school. For example, I know of at least two people who have become headteachers of the school where they started out as trainee teachers and there are doubtless many other examples around the country. I could not think of anything I would rather do less, but it clearly worked for them.

This book's strap-line talks of the challenges and rewards of school leadership. One of the major personal challenges for you as an individual is to keep track of where your career is and more importantly, where your thinking is at each stage of your working life. If you do not do this you will never experience the challenges and rewards of headship because you will in all likelihood never be appointed – self evident but true nonetheless. There is no proven established blueprint for how anyone will arrive in a senior leadership position. A career tends to be made up of a mix of careful planning, hard work, contextual circumstances, sudden realisations and not a little luck.

For example, one head told me that he had worked in boys' schools all his working life before deciding to apply for jobs in mixed comprehensives. He was also the father of four sons! Needless to say this fact counted against him on several interviews until he met a headteacher who happened to have four daughters. Part of their conversation over lunch on the first day of interviews centred on their combined inability to understand their children and the degree to which boys could behave like girls sometimes and vice versa!

He was convinced that that conversation gave him the edge over the other candidates and was a key reason why he was appointed to that particular post. It was a decision that was made by the head in spite of some vigorous opposition from other panel members who were worried by the obvious lack of relevant experience but in the final analysis the decision turned out to be the right one. Four years later he was appointed to the headship of a large mixed comprehensive where he enjoyed considerable success.

Maintaining a clear perspective

A recurring message from this example of career progression is the extent to which you have to maintain a very clear perspective on where you are and where you would like to be in five years' time, for example. It is fatally easy to move to a job which you enjoy, make friends, become very familiar and settled with the way the school is run and suddenly realise that you have been there for ten years! Even then you may well still find the role enjoyable and the tasks interesting and challenging but the key question for those who are mid-career and who will now be looking to retire in their late sixties is how to ensure that the latter stages of their time in teaching are just as rewarding as the first few years, and perhaps even more so.

One of the very real highlights for me has been taking on new roles that have, frankly, terrified me initially but have resulted in the realisation that I could do things that I had previously thought beyond me. A classic example of this was when I had to create a timetable back in the 1980s (long before computer programs appeared) for a large mixed comprehensive. As an English teacher who is much more comfortable with words than figures, I was utterly convinced that it was a job that I could not do and the first few weeks of planning and analysis gave me many sleepless nights. But the sense of achievement when I published my first timetable – and it actually worked – was huge and tangible. I genuinely did not think that I was capable of doing it. As it turned out I was actually really good at solving those seemingly insoluble problems that present themselves at the very end of a timetable's construction. I could not have been more surprised! On reflection, spending countless hours puzzling over what is in fact a deceptively addictive activity as well as having the good fortune to be mentored and supported in the early stages by a remarkably good timetabler/tutor, paid dividends.

Looking back over my career, I realise how much I would have missed out on and how much less I would have been able to develop and use skills (that I did not know I even possessed) if I had remained in jobs that I enjoyed at the time. Making yourself (and very often your family) move out of a familiar comfort zone is never easy but by doing this you are far more likely to give yourself many more opportunities to expand your knowledge and horizons than you ever would by just taking the easy option and staying in a comfortable job. To be honest, I have never been convinced that staying in the same job for 30 years or more was a great thing to do because there were 'always new challenges'. Real challenges come from changing schools and taking on new, more demanding roles that initially look extremely daunting but in the long run give you much greater job satisfaction and from which you learn far more about yourself as a person.

Talking heads

Celia, a head of a medium-sized primary school in the west of England in her early thirties, talks about the first five years of her teaching career:

To be honest, I felt about as 'ordinary' as you can be when I started teaching. Although I was reasonably clever and had a fair amount of street wisdom, I never considered myself to be academically able or particularly ambitious. I certainly didn't have great qualifications! Like so many other new teachers, I was most concerned with finding out whether I could cut it as a teacher and if I could win over the kids. You heard so many stories then about how hard and unappreciated teaching was as a job (frequently from experienced teachers!) and there were so many stories in the press about schools with no discipline and children apparently running riot that the last thing on my mind in the first couple of years was advancing my career. Survival was the over-riding concern!

And yet, much sooner than I would have envisaged, I started looking at people in my school who were holding down posts of responsibility and enjoying the challenge. I also saw some teachers who had been at the school for a very long time and had been doing the same job for as long as they could remember. I knew that in general the people in the first category were more positive and upbeat than the latter and that really resonated with me. From that moment on I started thinking seriously about what I wanted to do and how I might set about achieving some form of promotion. I never dreamt that I would become a headteacher at such a relatively young age but I knew that I was not going to let the grass grow under my feet and run the risk of becoming as disillusioned as some of my colleagues had so patently become in the later stages of their career.

Barriers to career progression

Celia's memories of older teachers having the potential to influence the new teachers is worth bearing in mind when thinking of your own career. There is no doubt that in some, if not most schools, there will be a group of staff who will regard anyone with any sense of purpose or ambition as being something of a threat. It is disheartening to observe young upbeat entrants to the profession become disgruntled and disillusioned by older staff who resent their enthusiasm and attempt to either turn them into clones of themselves or force them to leave the school to try to find a more sympathetic working environment elsewhere. This is particularly true if, and when, a head of department or year or middle leader whose own career has stalled or gone backwards, manages to create a sense in his/her department that 'challenge' is a dirty word, that being satisfactory is absolutely fine and that attempting to change or confront the status quo and improve the school is not what young teachers should do or are expected to do.

As a school leader, addressing this particular problem in order to improve the lot of teachers concerned is very hard and complex. This book is about coping with the reality of school leadership and it is a headteacher's duty to challenge underperformance and deal with staff who are not making a positive contribution to the life of the school. However, when a middle leader is competent enough but just not very good, all the forces of employment law seem to be stacked against you as a head. The process of removing poor middle leaders and teachers is so unnecessarily complex and energy-sapping that while you are dealing with the problem, there is a risk that more important aspects of your work will inevitably be put on the back burner. In my view, any head who tells you that she can get rid of staff who are not up to standard very quickly and easily is not telling you the truth. Dealing with difficult and underperforming teachers is demanding on your time and stress levels, time-consuming, frustrating, unpleasant and on occasions downright bloody.

There are two reasons for mentioning the barriers to career progression:

- Firstly, you need to be aware of how testing it can sometimes be to project and maintain an image of wanting to get on and make a success of your career.
- Secondly, when you do reach a senior leadership position in a school, you should not feel that you are the first person to come up against negative thinking or that you are the only headteacher who appears to be having trouble dealing with it.

In the best schools people regard career progression as sensible and right and not only encourage it but also help to make it happen. But not every school is a 'best school' and very often energetic and dynamic teachers are promoted to senior leadership positions in schools where there is much work to be done. In those situations it is wise to go into the job with your eyes as wide open as possible.

Preparing for headship: determining the future, creating the culture

It may appear far-fetched to suggest that anyone looking to move into a senior leadership role should be thinking about the implications and realities of doing so at the very start of their career, but I believe that in the best schools every member of staff is expected, and actively encouraged, to take on leadership roles as soon as they join the organisation. I know of some headteachers who advocate performance-review systems in their schools where they do not consider it right or valid for any member of staff who is not in a middle leadership position or higher to set leadership targets as part of their performance cycle. I have never subscribed to this view: young teachers taking control of a group of students are already engaged in a leadership role and they should be challenged and assessed accordingly. The most effective schools will always promote a leadership culture where everyone is a leader and where the roles and responsibilities will be determined far more by ability and ambition, and far less by age and the number of years they have been doing the job.

With this in mind, anyone entering teaching should be thinking very early on in their career how they can access the best and most relevant training in preparation for taking on leadership roles as soon as it becomes a realistic option. This does *not* mean that you automatically have to 'go on a course'. In fact, sometimes taking a course is the last thing you should do. It would be great to be able to say that all courses, run by a vast number of training providers, are brilliant and inspirational but many – too many in my experience – are anything but. Too often teachers will come back from training sessions saying that the best part of the programme by far was the talk with colleagues from other schools at coffee and lunch. This does not mean to say that training programmes are a waste of time – far from it. The secret is accessing the right leadership training for the right reasons at the right time.

How to access the best training

Finding the best training is not as difficult as it might at first appear. It is important to do your homework. Read training journals, read impartial assessments of training providers, all of which will provide examples of the quality of what they offer. It is relatively straightforward to gauge their own assessment of their work by seeking out independent reviews, much in the same way as you would Google a hotel recommended to you, to find out what it's really like. Ask people who have attended courses run by one particular provider whether they provide value for money. In fact, there is a wealth of information in any staffroom that will help you sift the inadequate from the very good.

The National College for School Leadership has, for example, during the course of its operations to date provided an exceptionally varied and wide-ranging programme of leadership training, the quality of which has necessarily and understandably varied. Some has been excellent (the research associate scheme and the fast track programme for outstanding new entrants to the profession for instance) and some has been far less well regarded. When the original version of NPQH (the National Professional Qualification for Headship) was introduced in the UK in 1997 as a training programme specifically geared for headship preparation, there were high hopes that it would be tailored to meet the specific needs and challenges presented by the role.

The reality was different: too often the people leading the training were not experienced practitioners or qualified enough to run courses at this level, the programmes of study were deemed to be too theoretical and narrowly focused but most significantly, far too many people accepted on the course were highly unlikely ever to be appointed to a headship. The latest, much-revised version of the qualification has listened to these criticisms and appears to be much more targeted, relevant and focused. The fact that it is no longer a compulsory qualification for anyone seeking headship will no doubt determine its fate: it will have to be good!

Unless you keep your ear to the ground and do your own research you will not develop a clear view on what training and preparation will work and will not work for you. Consider the following:

- Ask people whose opinions you respect and act on their advice. Do not assume that the member of staff who has responsibility for Continuing Professional Development will necessarily always know the best training for you. Talk to people and then make your own mind up.

- As a general rule, if you are looking to take an additional qualification, always choose a well-regarded leadership qualification such as an MBA or a master's level qualification in educational leadership at a leading, well-established university. It is very easy, for example, to find yourself spending a great deal of your spare time studying for a certificate or a programme of study that has been aggressively promoted by a local training body that within two years is not worth the paper it is written on.

- There are plenty of people who will pre-judge your suitability for specific training programmes. Very often these judgements will be influenced by age, gender etc. Be clear and unequivocal about your own agenda and ambitions and stay focused on them.

- Remember that the best training opportunities will be the ones that really test your abilities, stretch you and help you re-define your personal goals. The Talking head below illustrates this point very effectively.

Talking heads

Dave has been a headteacher of two very challenging secondary schools in the West Midlands, both of which were in special measures when he was appointed and both of which improved dramatically under his leadership. He recalled a training opportunity that made a real impact on him and his career.

I have always regarded professional development with a considerable degree of caution because, to be frank, I have been subjected to more than my fair share of sub-standard training that has left me feeling irritated and frustrated. As a deputy head in the early 1990s the problem was especially acute because of the paucity of high-quality headship training at the time. You can imagine how I felt when my head suggested quite strongly that I sign up for a weekend training course for headship run by a small training company operating in Solihull!

It turned out to be the best preparation for headship that I ever had. There were only 12 of us on the course and we were told at the start that there would be a fair amount of role play (which made my heart sink) but the basic idea for the weekend was original and powerful. The presenters created a school ('Longacres') which they told us was advertising for a new head. Day 1 of the course was a series of information gathering sessions for us as potential candidates for the post. The second day pitched all 12 of us against each other while we were put through a round of interviews and written tasks.

At the end of the day, an appointment was made and we then had extensive and very valuable feedback about where we had done well and where we needed to sharpen up. Although I was not successful on the day I found the whole experience invaluable and the feedback was brilliant: clear, perceptive and constructively critical. The fact the all the trainers were, or had been, headteachers of large secondary schools made it even more relevant and worthwhile. Such a simple, clever idea!

The cultural shift

There are two ways of developing your career: you can either let other people manage it or you can manage it yourself. I have seen many talented teachers lose out by being too reactive and as a consequence miss out on many opportunities to take on new challenges and perspectives. At my first school, ten newly qualified teachers started at the same time and over the next three years we were very aware that we were setting ourselves against each other in a spirit of fierce, albeit friendly, rivalry. The perceived wisdom then was:

- It was essential to gain some form of promotion in the first three years.
- You were strongly advised to spend a maximum of five years (three preferably) in your first school.
- You 'needed' to be in a middle leadership role by the time you were 30.
- If you hadn't made deputy headship by the time you were 40 you were unlikely to do so.

- Most headteachers secured their first post in their early forties. If you got to 50 without doing so, you were never going to.

I have never been certain where these so-called established truths came from but I do know they were common parlance in most staffroom conversations in the early days of my career. I remember being extremely relieved when I finally got my career moving in some sort of direction at the end of my second year of teaching, when I was awarded the responsibility for editing the school magazine! It may well have been the case that in the UK in the early 1970s because teaching was so poorly paid, teachers believed (quite rightly) that promotion was just about the only way of securing a half decent income. Mike, one of our interviewees, openly admits that a major motivator in his drive to become a head was in part a response to the fact that he had a wife and four small children and needed to provide for them.

The situation today is very different and there is no doubt that teaching has a higher perceived status, as a well regarded profession among the public than it did 30 years ago. Many more people are attracted to teaching because they see a job that will challenge them and provide a degree of personal satisfaction that they cannot find elsewhere. The UK's Graduate Teacher Programme (now sadly defunct) has been one of the most effective recruiting agents of the last 30 years in this regard and has brought into schools large numbers of very talented graduates from many different spheres of work. In my own time as a head, I was both delighted and astonished at the number and quality of the graduates we interviewed for graduate trainee teacher posts. Each year we had well over 300 strong applications for 20 places: research chemists, chartered engineers, high-flying accountants and financial traders, doctors, architects, surveyors and dentists – all looking to enter a profession that they felt would give them a reasonable income, good promotion prospects and a greater sense of vocation.

I do think that in the UK there has been a shift in the way entrants to the profession view their potential career path. Many newly qualified teachers seem quite content to learn their craft and make no real efforts to gain any form of promotion until several years after they have started. Many others have taken a significant cut in salary to enter teaching and although money is of course still a factor, job satisfaction is paramount. However, unlike graduate entrants 30 years ago, graduates no longer see it as a job for life. This is by no means confined to teaching: Cappelli (1999, p.148) considers that 'career jobs are in decline'. Many graduates obtain a teaching qualification, do the job for a number of years and then move on to something else. The fact that quite a large number of people are coming into teaching as mature entrants means that the conventional career profile no longer applies. As a result, you now have people being appointed to first headships in their thirties, forties and fifties and second headships in their sixties.

The unwritten but widely accepted 'rules' quoted earlier no longer seem to exist in such stark form. However, there are still certain realities that you need to bear in mind when considering your own career and your chances of securing the top job. For example, if you have not secured some form of leadership responsibility within five years of obtaining your first post, future bosses may interpret this as a lack of ambition. Similarly, if you stay in the same school for a very long time, your chances of promotion at another school will in all likelihood be adversely affected. Remember as well that, the majority of high-flying entrants to the profession will have reached senior leadership level by their mid to late thirties at the latest and that the most difficult promotional stage by far is the move from head of department and/or assistant headship to deputy headship because applications can come from such a wide variety of sources. After deputy headship the number of applications (as you approach the top of the pyramid) is much smaller nowadays – a point discussed in more detail in Chapter 3.

Pause for thought

- Bear in mind that if you do stay in your first school for a long time it will make securing a promoted post at another school increasingly difficult. It will be even more difficult if you move from the state to the private sector because the longer you stay, the harder it will be to make the move back.
- More and more candidates for senior leadership positions in schools have a post-graduate qualification in educational leadership. Some have more! Where does that place you and your chances of securing promotion?
- Although, as I said earlier, the hard and fast rule about making headship before your fiftieth birthday no longer applies, it is still preferable to do so. Apart from anything else it gives you the option to move out of school leadership or on to a second/third headship.
- You need to be weighing up all these factors when you are mapping out your own career and it is vital that you are regularly and candidly re-defining your own targets and aspirations.

Talking heads

Dominic, the head of a medium sized comprehensive on the south coast, talked about a significant episode in his own career.

I rather foolishly, in hindsight, moved from a grammar school in Surrey to a leadership position in the English department of what was at the time an 11–18 technical school. Two years after I joined the school, the county (Kent) underwent some re-organisation and the school became a grammar school. As a result, I spent the first 14 years of my career in selective boys' schools. Unsurprisingly, even though I was promoted fairly rapidly to the position of assistant head ('senior teacher' as it was then) my subsequent applications for deputy headships in mixed comprehensive schools clearly and understandably went straight in the bin. I knew I had to do something pretty dramatic if I was not to become trapped. Much as I enjoyed the school, I did not relish the thought of spending the rest of my working life there. The head was sympathetic to my plight and when I suggested the possibility of doing a one-year exchange to a mixed comprehensive he did not dismiss the idea out of hand.

Very fortunately for me, he had a conversation with a fellow head a couple of weeks later who told him he had a member of his English department who was desperate for promotion but who had never taught A level. As a result of this conversation the exchange was set up and went ahead the following term. I absolutely loved my time at the school. Interestingly, one of the best aspects of the experience was the opportunity it gave me to get back to the day job of teaching a full timetable, being a form tutor and having the time to concentrate on honing and improving my teaching skills. Two months after my return, I was shortlisted for a deputy headship of a very large mixed comprehensive and was appointed to the post. My new head told me afterwards that if I had not done the exchange there was no way I would have been shortlisted. I am absolutely convinced that if I hadn't forced the issue and been supported by a great headteacher, I would in all probability still be teaching at the same school today. And how much I would have missed!

The importance of being proactive

A big mistake made by some people is to spend too much time waiting for things to happen or assuming that the perfect job will somehow magically appear out of the ether. While they are waiting, they make little or no attempt to fine-tune their skills and experiences or access any and all opportunities to improve and enhance their career profile. People who are successful in any walk of life invariably have to work with single-minded determination and bounce back from the inevitable setbacks and knocks that appear to go hand in hand with ambition.

Anti-stagnation

Dominic's account is an excellent example of how, by being positive and proactive, you can make things happen and avoid a stale working life. There are people who advance their careers by being ruthlessly single-minded and ambitious, and there is nothing wrong with that as long as other people do not get bulldozed along the way. Other people advance their careers because they have a sixth sense about when they are (if not actually) losing interest in their work; they are aware that they have lost the 'buzz' that gets them up in the morning.

There are two ways of dealing with this feeling. You can keep pushing it to the back of your mind, take on additional challenges in your current school and convince yourself that these feelings of restlessness and unease will pass. Surely, if you wait long enough something will come along that will appeal to you and you will take the plunge and move school then. Adopting that approach will almost certainly mean that you end up doing nothing and you will spend the rest of your career at that school. If that works for you, fine, but if it is not really what you want, the latter stages of your working life will be at least tinged (and probably filled) with regret.

The other way of dealing with it is to recognise and accept that the feeling is not going to go away by itself and therefore you must begin to construct a game plan which will propel you into applying for new jobs. The need to be proactive is once again paramount and this includes looking for newer and better ways of accessing the best training for you. As has already been said, attending courses, taking additional qualifications, reading journals and any of the vast number of books on leadership are all well and good but if you are really determined to advance your career you also need to be more imaginative and innovative about how you learn more about the skills needed to take on senior leadership roles.

Taking control of your career

Talk to people who have a proven track record

Talking to leaders who have already proved that they are very good at transforming schools may seem an obvious thing to suggest but I have met a number of aspiring headteachers who have never done this. If you think the head at your own particular school is not very good, find out who the best heads in the area are and do whatever it takes to meet them and pick their brains. Most heads, given half the chance, are delighted to talk about their philosophy, their experience, what works for them and what does not. You can learn so much from these conversations. I have known a lot of teachers who, when studying for masters' qualifications, have said that the research they had to carry out for their dissertations has been immensely valuable. Frequently, as the qualification suggests, the people interviewed are head/deputy headteachers and if the research requires you to interview ten or more senior leaders, the body of evidence you end up with is significant.

Work shadowing

There is no better training for headship, in my view, than work shadowing someone who is really experienced and very effective in their role. Again, I have met very few people who are looking to become heads who have actually done this. If you have a very understanding and sympathetic head in your own school there is every possibility that he or she will arrange for you to do some work shadowing. There are also leadership courses, notably those run by the National College, that are increasingly looking to include work sharing/shadowing in the course programme. The most beneficial aspect of this form of training is that you are much more likely to learn about the reality of school leadership than you are about the theory. Practising heads who have achieved great things in their own careers are, usually more than willing to share their views on what makes the job as exciting, frustrating and as challenging as it is and shadowing them for a day or a week or even longer is invaluable professional development because it allows you to experience the reality rather than the rhetoric of school leadership.

Rotating responsibilities

Many leadership teams operate schemes whereby roles and responsibilities are regularly rotated. I am certain this provides excellent professional development for the team. It is also, as far as the head is concerned, a clever and effective way of sifting out the less ambitious and least hard working members of the team who will nearly always prefer to carry on doing jobs they are very familiar with. I have known assistant heads in schools who have done the timetable for 30 years and never tire of it. Unsurprisingly, they have never shown any interest in working anywhere else or moving up to the next rung of the leadership ladder.

However, if you are ambitious, being able to list a wide range of whole-school responsibilities on your CV will make you a much stronger candidate and give you much more confidence when it comes to the interview stage of the selection process. Doing the timetable for a whole school, for instance, is not only an interesting intellectual challenge, it also provides invaluable insights into how a curriculum works and presents you with numerous opportunities to refine your negotiating and diplomatic skills when it comes to dealing with middle/senior leaders, all of whom have their own particular needs and demands. But don't do it for 30 years! Other areas which give you the same 'whole-school' perspective include professional development, professional review, whole-school budgetary responsibilities, pastoral leadership and international perspectives.

Keeping yourself professionally fit

If you are genuinely ambitious and determined to advance your career, you need to keep up to date with what is going on in the world of education and be ready to go for a particular job when it comes up. However, far too many people make the mistake of doing very little by way of preparation until that particular job is advertised and assume they can simply put in an application and be appointed to the post. I have met colleagues who, although they have not applied for a post anywhere for several years, are surprised and disappointed when they are not automatically shortlisted when they eventually get round to putting in an application for a headship. I have interviewed a number of candidates for senior leadership posts who arrive for the interview hopelessly unprepared and ill informed. Some do not even bother to find out basic information about the school and are surprised when you ask them what they thought of the school's most recent Ofsted report – even though it was included in the information pack!

At the start of this chapter mention was made of the number of people who talk but do not walk a successful career. Even though I have interviewed a number of heads who did not set out on their career intending to run their own school, I have never interviewed successful and well-regarded school leaders who were not passionate about education, incredibly hard working and single-minded in their determination to do best by the students and staff of their school. Maybe it was that passion and single-mindedness together with an unrelenting fear of stagnation that made them move from one challenge to the next.

If you are fortunate enough to work for a head who embraces and practises distributive leadership there is every possibility that you will be given a range of challenging whole-school responsibilities. The best heads also delegate properly and make people accountable for their actions. They give members of their leadership team tasks to carry out, they expect their team members to carry them out, give appropriate support and guidance and welcome and act on the opinions of and feedback from their team. By so doing, they create a can-do culture. If you are unlucky enough to work for a head who does none of these things then you need to move school! The most important thing is to do whatever it takes to avoid that creeping sense of becoming stale because it can wield such a corrosive and damaging influence on the levels of job satisfaction.

Conclusion

No matter how determined you are there is, of course, no guarantee that you will secure a headship. For example, there are approximately 600,000 teachers in the UK and only 25,000 schools so the odds of securing a headship from the outset are not high! In my career I met many talented teachers who had all the necessary skills and professional commitment to become highly effective school leaders but for whatever reason it never happened. Equally, I have met quite a few headteachers who have not, in my view, been anywhere near as talented as teachers so there is no doubt that context and good fortune (see Chapter 10) can play a highly significant part in determining your career. However, if by any chance a headship escapes you, it is vitally important to make sure that you continue to develop as a person and as a practitioner and look to take on any leadership roles that come your way.

Action points

- Regularly review, update and improve your CV and make sure that your letter of application is as good as it can be and is specifically targeted at the school you are planning to put in an application for. Let people whose opinions you value look at both documents, and make an effort to respond to their constructive criticisms and advice.
- Look rigorously and consistently for job opportunities that might suit your strengths and aspirations and, unless it is unavoidable, do not restrict yourself to one particular part of the geographical area.

- Always be willing to take on new roles and responsibilities even if the tasks themselves do not really enthuse you. Headship requires you to know a great deal about how a school operates and that means becoming well versed in areas of its operation that do not necessarily interest you.

- Volunteer at regular intervals for mock interviews and ask for detailed and honest feedback on your strengths and weaknesses. Take every opportunity to seek out the views and advice of people who you know are very good headteachers.

- Apply for jobs that are not, as far as you are concerned, the 'perfect fit'. If you are lucky enough to be shortlisted, the experience of being interviewed for a senior leadership role is invaluable and you may find yourself really liking a school that on paper looked very unpromising. It happened to me!

3 The challenges and rewards of headship

Chapter overview

This chapter addresses the following:

- Why people are drawn to headship: the motives and the triggers.
- Why it is not an option for many people.
- Routes to headship.
- The excitement, the frustration and the fulfilment that the role offers.
- Initial challenges/opportunities.

Starting out

Why some people are attracted to headship

If you look at how and why some people arrive at headship, it may help to clarify whether or not you want the job and if you do, what might help you get it. In Chapter 10 we discuss some of the wide-ranging implications of the role that we hope will help you rationalise your thoughts and help you to reach a decision about what actions, if any, to take. For some people, the realisation that they want to run their own school cements the conviction that it is, for them, the right thing to aspire to. Where this conviction comes from depends on the circumstances and the individual. Some heads have said that it was a gradual acknowledgement as opposed to some kind of dramatic epiphany. Not one of them told me that they suddenly woke one morning, sat bolt upright in bed and exclaimed, 'I want to run my own school!' Instead, it tends to be a nagging conviction that grows stronger with the passing of time.

None of the headteachers interviewed said that they regretted taking on headship – in itself a powerful and compelling argument for considering the position. It was seen as an all-consuming job insofar as the hours were generally long and unforgiving, the pressures could, on occasions, be considerable and it was not a job you could leave at the school gate. Almost all of those people said that they rarely switched off and interestingly, no one considered that to be a problem.

Thinking about the job, trying to sort out a thorny problem, being in any number of different situations that gave you food for thought for a possible idea or innovation to introduce in to your own school was very much part of the territory of headship – and part of the fun! It seems to be the case that good headteachers actually relish the opportunity to talk about their work at weekends, evenings etc. to anyone who is vaguely interested in what they are doing. Partners are also very important in this regard: wives/husbands/girlfriends/boyfriends were important sounding boards and extremely influential guides and mentors.

The challenges: the exhilarating and the frustrating!

There is no doubt of course, that from time to time being a head can be the most frustrating and exasperating of jobs. The pace, the variety, the irritations, the physical and emotional pressures, the highs and lows clearly make the job what it is. There is no doubt either that the role is people-centred. Unfortunately, the bureaucratic demands, the inevitable paperwork, the need to keep up to date with important initiatives and new developments mean that if you are not careful you could spend all of your time sitting in your office in front of a computer. The best heads never allow this to happen, however, even if it means taking shortcuts with the paperwork finding a way to alleviate the external pressures put on them. Instead, they make sure that they are out and about in their schools talking to staff and students, keeping up to date with what is happening in terms of staff morale, and keeping an ear to the ground to assess the success, or otherwise, of work that is being done and new initiatives that are being put in place. Good heads pick up a lot about the feel of their schools from the corridor conversations (see Chapter 5) and these are so important in order to keep in touch with what is going well and what is not.

Talking heads

Gill, a relatively young head of a medium-sized mixed comprehensive who has been in the job for five years articulated a common theme:

> It's a job like no other. There are times when things get so difficult you want to scream but you know that if you do, it has to be in a closed room where no one, apart from possibly your PA, can hear you. Some staff (albeit a minority) can be so difficult: they mistrust because you are seen as 'management' and therefore devious and out to get them. No matter what you try to do it never seems to appease them and even when you seem to be offering help and advice it is greeted with suspicion. However, you can be having a tough day and then you walk in to an assembly and see some of your students doing a terrific sales pitch for a charity they are supporting and you feel so proud you could burst! It can be an emotional roller coaster but the opportunities you have to make a difference, a real difference to the life chances of young people make it a job like no other. Now that I've been a head for five years I couldn't imagine doing anything else.

Why some people manage to secure headships

Working for heads who challenge

Some headteachers have been inspired to run their own schools by working with an inspirational headteacher who has encouraged them to apply for the position because they are convinced that they have the intellect, the tenacity and personality to be successful in the role. Occasionally this encouragement is more implicit than overt.

Talking heads

Mike, a headteacher in the south of England, discussed the factors that made him determined to be a head:

> The first was prosaic and somewhat unusual: a young father of four children with a wife who was at home running the family meant that I needed to be

earning as much money as I could as quickly as possible! I was therefore a young, ambitious teacher in a hurry, keen to gain promotion as soon as possible. Inevitably (in retrospect), I came into conflict with my first headteacher.

I'm sure he found my apparent (I hope!) arrogance and self-assurance tiresome at times. I thought I was being enthusiastic and constructive and could not understand why he did not automatically agree with everything I was proposing. Looking back on that time I now realise why he found me so trying. However, on one occasion he stopped a heated debate I was having with him in the corridor about yet another initiative I was attempting to sell him and said that when I was a head I would understand why it was not a viable option and then walked off. The fact that he said 'when' not 'if' had a tremendous effect on me. His implicit acknowledgement that I would one day run my own school gave me the impetus and the belief to go for headship. I will never forget that.

Paul, a headteacher in the north of England, looked back fondly on his time as a deputy head working with a head whom he came to admire greatly:

My boss and I did mad crazy things. We were encouraged to think the impossible, to be change agents. I learnt so much about monitoring/evaluation and teaching and learning. I was particularly influenced by seeing how motivational education could be. We did a great deal of work on quality in the classroom. Invaluable.

Dave, another head who works in the Midlands remembers the head he worked with when he was a senior teacher:

She made Margaret Thatcher look like (Little) Bo Peep. You were either petrified or in awe of her – or both! I was in awe, but not frightened. I learnt from her never to accept the status quo, always have the highest standards, always remember that you can do things without compromising your principles. She took me to levels of leadership I had not been to before.

Working in the right leadership culture

Another significant factor is the cultural context in which you are or were working as a deputy or member of the senior leadership team. Some headteachers, when they are planning for deputy heads to join their leadership teams, are looking to appoint safe, fairly conventional people who will not rock the boat, will not challenge the status quo and who will probably want to remain in post for the rest of their working careers. Other heads however, will be keen to appoint people they feel instinctively have the ability and the drive to become headteachers. These heads will not want their deputies to stay for more than five years at the most and will be expecting them to challenge the established practices of the school and, where appropriate, disagree clearly and robustly with ideas being proposed by the head if they consider them to be unwise or poorly thought through.

Two days after I was appointed to a deputy headship in a large, rural mixed comprehensive in Kent, the head asked me to walk the building and make a list of all the things I thought were odd, unclear or, in my view, plain wrong:

> Ask me anything you like about what we do here. I don't care if it turns out to be a daft question and do not for one second think I am going to be offended if you believe we've got some things fundamentally wrong. I need your fresh eyes and I need your honesty.

I took him at his word and the head was true to his.

The working relationship between us was professionally fulfilling and stimulating. Even more important, this particular head's determination to question constantly the relevance and value of what was done at the school and empower his leadership team to develop, lead and implement school-wide innovations provided me with tremendous professional development and first-class preparation for taking the next step. Unsurprisingly, during this head's long and distinguished tenure at the school, 11 deputy heads secured headships.

Motivation: the wrong and the right role model!

Conversely, other people have been compelled to apply for headship because they have worked for headteachers they consider to be hopelessly ineffective. Barry, a highly regarded and successful executive headteacher in the north of England, remembers the head he worked for:

> She was an appalling head – the most incompetent, irrational, damaging and dangerous person I have ever encountered in education. She damaged good teachers' careers because of her cross behaviour. The staff spent all the time in a state of siege. I spent six years perpetually angry and frustrated but I learnt so much about people management by witnessing so dramatically how not to do it.

Although Barry's experience is extreme, it is by no means uncommon for heads to admit that the major driving force to run their own schools came from seeing other people do it ineffectively and convincing themselves that they could, given the opportunity, be so much better in the role.

Proactively avoiding frustration

A number of people interviewed for this book commented that reaching deputy headship was both an achievement in itself and a major incentive for wanting to secure the top job. Certainly, although David and I each worked as deputies for successful and supportive heads, we both felt that we would have been ultimately deeply frustrated if we never had been given the opportunity to try to run our own schools and put into practice some deeply cherished ideas.

Talking heads

Diane, a mature entrant to the profession, became a head of a federation of primary schools in her late fifties. She qualified shortly before her fortieth birthday and began teaching at a medium-sized primary school.

Even though I was perfectly happy in my work, I wanted a headship because I wanted to engineer a school to reflect my own firmly held beliefs about what works well and what does not. My experience of working as a senior manager in British Gas for over ten years prior to qualifying as a teacher gave me, I believe, the confidence and the skill-set to take on headship. I was successful on my third attempt and after only one year in post, I was offered the chance to take on another small school as a federation head, an offer I found irresistible and which turned out to be the most challenging and fulfilling period in my teaching career.

The lucky break

Most texts on leadership will tell you that one element that is consistent in all successful careers is luck and this is especially true when it comes to securing a headship. Alex, a very successful and highly-regarded deputy head at a boys' selective school in Kent, posted two applications for headships on the same day

– one to a traditional mixed grammar school in Dorset and an identical application to an almost identical school in Lincolnshire. Even though it was patently clear that he was an exceptionally strong candidate for both posts, the outcome was dramatically different. His application to the school in Dorset was not even acknowledged but the following week he was appointed head of the school in Lincolnshire.

There are other factors regarding interviews for headship which could be regarded as the luck of the draw. Although it will of course never be mentioned in public, gender preferences may work for or against you. If you are a woman and the governors are bidding farewell to a female head who has been sensational in the role then there is every possibility that you will have a slight advantage over the other candidates. Despite selection panels being adamant that they are looking for the best person regardless of gender, the reality is that on many occasions they will be thinking in their own minds that they would prefer a woman or a man depending on individual contexts. Then again, sometimes you can come up against a truly outstanding candidate who comes with an impressive track record, who doesn't put a foot wrong over the two (sometimes three) days of interview and fits the school like a glove. In that case the only correct form of action is to be philosophical and take what you can from the experience.

Luck was very much in evidence when David applied for a headship in Northamptonshire. The feedback he received from day one of his interview was very positive and he was shortlisted to go through to the second day as one of only three remaining candidates. The second day went well too and David was fairly confident that if the final interview with a small panel of governors and senior officers from the local authority was successful, he would be in the frame for the post.

Not long into this final interview, he was asked by the Chair of Governors if there were any central issues about the school that he would be looking to address if he was appointed headteacher, and what would he be looking to do in the first month. David began to answer the question by saying that there were one or two aspects of the school that had rung alarm bells in his own mind when he was walking the site. At that precise moment, the school bell rang for change of lesson. David smiled broadly at the panel, held his hands up and said 'Do you need any more?' He is convinced that this moment of pure chance sealed the decision in his favour.

Internal promotion

Being appointed internally to a headship can also be attributed, in part, to luck. There are occasions when a deputy head, for example, is propelled in to applying for a headship earlier than anticipated because a headship vacancy at their school suddenly becomes available and they know they cannot afford to miss out on the opportunity. Some deputy heads (occasionally very early in post) are presented with this extremely difficult scenario where they lose their headteacher. There could of course be a number of reasons: sudden unexpected promotion, long-term stress, illness, death in post, dismissal, secondment etc.

Although the prospect of taking up a role for which you have no direct training or expertise is initially daunting, very few people who have taken on headship in this way have ever had cause to regret having been given the opportunity. Many confirm what we have already suggested in this chapter – that the best preparation for headship is actually doing the job. A significant number of these acting heads end up being appointed to the permanent position and become fine, highly-regarded heads.

Dogged persistence!

I have already made reference in Chapter 2 to the extent to which some people really want to seek out headship, those who talk a lot in the staffroom about wanting the top job and then never apply for the post, and those who are convinced that securing a headship is a matter of 'when' not 'if'. However, a common theme running through most conversations with practising headteachers is the determination, single(bloody)-mindedness and perseverance that went into the business of securing first a deputy headship (in some ways a more difficult objective bearing in mind the nature, number and range of potential applicants) and subsequently a headship. As soon as you hear people saying that they did not apply for a particular post because it was a January start ('Nobody moves at Christmas') or an April start ('I can't possibly leave my students at such a crucial time of the year') or that the school is not quite the right age range or is not in precisely the right part of the country or their own children's education will suffer if they move any time over the next two/three years, you know that their heart is not really in it. Likewise, you will hear from some people, 'Of course, I could have been a head but…'. Need I say more?

Some people who are keen to become heads will apply every week for jobs. They will accept advice from any and all quarters about their CV, their letter of application, and their professional development needs. They will seek out and learn from experienced mentors and practising heads and undertake mock interviews with people they rate. They will be prepared to move at any time of the year and will have discussed with their wives or husbands and children which parts of the country are off the agenda, for whatever reason, and then apply for anything and everything that looks remotely challenging and attractive.

I vividly remember applying for deputy headships in mixed comprehensives when I had spent far too long as a senior teacher in a boys' selective school. I put in 72 applications over a period of 18 months (sometimes as many as six a week, all tailored to meet the specific requirements of each school), was long listed 28 times and only shortlisted once. Fortunately, I was offered the job after that one interview. When it came to headship, David and I both left wonderful schools in an area of the country we loved to take up headships and uprooted our families to parts of the country we did not love at all. It would have been so easy, and indeed was terribly tempting, to find all those laudable and plausible excuses for not accepting these jobs – and how much we would have both missed out on if we had!

Pause for thought

- Do not assume that there is only one route to headship or that you need to be a particular sort of person to consider applying for the job. Bear in mind that headteachers arrive in posts from all directions, in all shapes, personalities and sizes and from many different backgrounds.
- There is no reason to be discouraged or intimidated by people who claim to be natural heads and who never appear to doubt their ability. In my view, the vast majority are lacking in emotional intelligence and will rarely, if ever, be good headteachers.
- Do not be deterred by people who claim that career breaks occasioned by bringing up a family preclude you from headship. They don't.
- The more heads you talk to, the more stories you will hear about how and why they ended up running their own schools. Learn from them!

Issues to consider when thinking about headship

Is it really worth the effort?

The fact that there is a serious shortage of those who want the job in a number of developed countries is evidenced by the worrying fall in the number of applicants for headships or principalships at all levels in the education sector. There is no doubt that a major factor affecting the dramatic reduction in the number of people applying for headships over the last decade is directly attributable to the rise in the public accountability of schools and the increasingly punitive and destructive judgements of external auditing agencies such as Ofsted, the inspectorate service in England and Wales.

Of course, by definition headship has never been easy but nonetheless, in the UK in the early 1990s, it was not unusual for schools to receive very large numbers of applications for a headship position. When I obtained my first headship (at a tough school in a 'difficult' area in the Midlands) there were well over 100 applications and ten people with substantial senior leadership experience were shortlisted. When I applied ten years later to a much larger, nationally-recognised flagship comprehensive school in the Midlands with more than 2,000 students on roll and where the governors were offering an exceptionally generous financial package, there were 19 applications and a shortlist of just six.

To address this growing problem, many initiatives have been put in place by central governments and by local or regional authorities to make headship more accessible and attractive and increase the number of appropriately equipped and qualified recruits. The number of leadership programmes for aspiring heads, newly appointed heads, heads who have been in post for some years and those experienced heads who want federation or consultant headship, training has expanded significantly over the last 15 years. Other initiatives in the UK have included fast track professional development programmes like Teach First and Future Leaders for young teachers who are identified as high flyers with the potential to move into senior leadership roles, most likely in challenging schools, within five years of starting out.

In spite of all such schemes and innovations recruitment, certainly in the UK, is probably much worse than it was even five years ago and currently shows little or no real signs of improving – this in spite of the dramatic rise in the range and number of professional development opportunities targeted at aspiring heads, the various attempts to spot and nurture talented teachers and the significant increase in headteacher salaries.

Do I need the pressures and responsibilities?

In line with this trend, there is an increasingly large number of deputy heads currently in post who have no intention of taking on the additional stresses and responsibilities of headship because they do not perceive it to be worth the sacrifice, the commitment or the hassle. One highly-regarded headteacher of an outstanding large mixed comprehensive school in Somerset attributes much of the success the school has enjoyed over the last 15 years to the work of his long serving first class deputies, none of whom has any intention of applying for headships. 'Why should they?' he said. 'They get all the excitement and satisfaction of leadership without the ultimate weariness of knowing you are where the buck stops.'

The responsibilities of headship have always been wide-ranging and considerable and the job has inevitably always required high levels of resilience, passion and commitment. However, the expectations and levels of scrutiny that now go hand in hand with the role are very different. A headteacher 30 years ago, would neither be expected to or even begin to recognise the range and diversity of the work a school leader has to deal with today. The headteacher of a school David and I both worked in during the 1970s was perfectly competent and approachable but each year he would fill in his yearly diary almost exclusively by copying what he had put in for the year before. The school play, reports, parents' evenings, speech days – all would be the same events on the same days with more often than not most of the same people organising them, because staff turnover was very low.

Nowadays, the pressures in the UK in terms of personal and professional accountability have increased year on year since the introduction of league tables and as a consequence, open (occasionally fairly hostile) competition has arisen between schools. Alongside this, the financial implications that are so dramatic when a drop in the number on roll, for example, of 50 students in a large secondary school in one financial year can result in a significant sum of money being taken from the budget, have made headteachers increasingly vulnerable.

Unsurprisingly, there has been a significant increase in the number of heads taking early retirement, leaving the post after a short time or being eased out by governing bodies who, somewhat like Premier League football clubs, believe that a change of manager will solve the problem of serial underachievement. It is hardly surprising therefore that fewer and fewer people are looking to take on the risks and expectations associated with the job.

Are you ambitious – honestly?

Over the last 30 years David and I have interviewed hundreds of young teachers entering the profession, teachers applying for heads of department, heads of faculty, heads of year posts and teachers applying for senior team leadership positions. Only a tiny minority of those have expressed any real interest in becoming headteachers. You can ask them if they are ambitious and if they say they are, you can ask them whether they eventually want to run their own schools.

It is surprising how few will be clearly focused in their determination to achieve that particular objective. Almost all of them say that they love teaching and that they have gained more personal and professional job satisfaction (especially the more mature entrants coming from other occupations into teaching mid-career) from working in schools than from any other occupation.

Most of these teachers however, do not tend to think very much about how their careers will develop over the next ten to 20 years; they definitely do not occupy much if any of their time considering whether or not they want to be headteachers running their own schools. When I began teaching it was widely assumed that it would be a job for life (see Chapter 2) and the ultimate ambition for some was to become a headteacher, but nowadays new entrants to the profession are much more guarded and uncertain even about how long they will teach for let alone what their ultimate ambition is.

At present, for example, the average time a qualified teacher in the UK stays in teaching is eight years. Most therefore will be setting their sights on learning their craft, accessing some relevant professional development and perhaps taking on a middle leadership role sometime within the first five to eight years. Very few will be seriously considering headship and even those teachers who have been in the job for over 15 years will rarely, if ever, give you a straight answer to the question 'Do you want to be a head?' This shift in emphasis might go some way to explaining why fewer people are considering whether headship is right for them. It would also explain why the majority of teachers do not even consider applying for headships until they are seasoned professionals with a wealth of middle/ senior leadership experience behind them.

Of course there have always been hundreds of perfectly justified reasons why people do not want to be a head: the hours, the stress, the thought of missing the teaching and the contact with the students, the overt and covert criticism from all sides, being under the public microscope, the accountability, the isolation, the at times ridiculous expectations – the list is almost endless! Many, if not most, of the people putting forward all the negative aspects of headship will, in all probability, never apply for the position. That level of responsibility and account-ability is just not for them whatever the appeal or the apparent rewards.

What finally convinces people?

Taking the plunge

The majority of those who do aspire to being a head will still in all probability be made up of those teachers who began their career determined to stay in teaching, made a success of each opportunity as it arose, avoided the complacency and potential stagnation which can come from staying in one post for too long and rose through the ranks to a senior leadership position from where the move to headship becomes an automatic, near inevitable final step. Taking that final step will trigger the sorts of questions, fears and apprehensions that should go through any sensible person's mind when thinking about headship:

- Do I need the additional hassle?
- Is it worth the extra money?
- Why I am entertaining the idea of moving out of my comfort zone?
- How will my family cope with the inevitable physical and mental upheaval?
- Will I be able to take a career break and still find the time and the energy to apply for a headship?
- Can I do the job as well as my current boss?
- Will I turn out to be as bad as my current boss?
- Is the stress as bad as they claim?
- If it is, will I be able to deal with it?

- Why are so many of my friends telling me I must be mad even to think of doing such a thing?
- What if I discover, too late, that I am completely out of my depth?

Two observations: first, this list could be considerably longer and secondly, just about everybody who has any sense or emotional intelligence will go through the same level of angst – not only when they are applying for headship but also when they are being interviewed, when they have been appointed and most probably in the first couple of years of actually doing the job. As a newly-appointed head talking to other headteachers who appear to you to be so comfortable in the role and so knowledgeable about virtually every-thing, the realisation that in amidst the pleasure and occasional euphoria they still experience moments of self doubt, depression and occasional despair is reassuring!

Talking heads

Bryn, a very successful and well-regarded head of a medium-sized grammar school in Kent was asked by a friend (who was also a teacher) how he felt after two years in the job, 'I'm a very good actor,' he said.

Most of my staff probably think I am exceedingly confident and very comfortable in the role but I do in fact find a great deal of it very hard and demanding. There are undoubted benefits and privileges and there are moments, quite a few moments in fact, when there is no other job I would ever want to do. The truth is, however, that I am nowhere near as confident as I appear. In fact, on more than a few occasions I feel like a newly qualified teacher pretending to be a headteacher just waiting to be found out!

The more you interview headteachers about how and why they considered taking on headship, the more diverse the reasons and the motives become. For example, if you ask any number of heads what they believe to be the toughest job (certainly physically) in a school they will say being a deputy head! The role is exceptionally challenging because it requires so many different skills, operating as it does in our view between whole-school decision making and working at the chalk face.

Andrew, recently retired, who in his career had five headships remarked:

I had no real ambition to be a head. Other people's incompetence drove me on. I saw them messing up a job and decided I must be able to do it as least as incompetently as they were. Being a deputy head was really difficult though. It was like having a hat without the feathers – lots of power and authority in one context, but in the business of real organisational change, not very much at all. It was exhausting! I only managed it for two and a half years and moved into headship with as much a sense of relief as elation.

Andrew was echoing a feeling expressed by many headteachers; although it carries considerable clout, being a deputy head does not give you that ultimate authority and that can be hard. For example, disagreeing fundamentally with your boss behind closed doors about a policy decision that you think will create many more problems than it will solve and then having to defend it doggedly in the staffroom (because that is your job) is very difficult! Most headteachers I have met said that deputy headship is a job most of us can only do well for a finite period of time and that sooner rather than later, applying for a headship becomes increasingly attractive for very many of them.

The vast majority of the heads I interviewed said that their careers were in no way carefully mapped out from day one; in fact, the major reason they went for promotion was less the attraction of the additional responsibility but more the desire to avoid getting stuck in their current role. This can be a tough position to be in, especially if even though you are currently happy in a leadership role in a school where you are settled and where your family is happy and secure, you still have the nagging conviction that you will miserable if you are in the same job five years down the line. We have already talked about successful deputies in well-run schools who work with inspirational heads but who have no desire to take on a headship themselves. They will not have the nagging doubts. If you do, then you will inevitably end up applying for a headship even if you are not at all sure that it is a sensible thing to do!

Arriving in post

The early challenges/demands

When you are starting out it is very easy to assume that every head you meet has got the job tapped, manages everything effortlessly, has an encyclopaedic grasp of all aspects of the role and appears to have a word-perfect recollection of every government innovation, diktat or education bill since the beginning of time. Going to a headteachers' conference, for example, can be an interesting experience. There are many great characters to be met but you can find yourself asking the question about some of the others: can these people *really* be like that? Or is this how they think they should behave and talk because they believe that is how headteachers are meant to behave and talk?'

I remember, at the age of 44, three weeks after taking up my first headship, when I went to my first headteachers' meeting I felt about 12 years old. Allowing for this slight exaggeration, it really is disconcerting to meet people who appear to be so comfortable and grown up in the role. I vividly recall that as I watched the head, who had been elected chair for the academic year and who was managing the meeting with such self-assurance and aplomb, I was absolutely convinced that even if I did the job for the next 50 years I would never be able to do what she was doing.

Preparing a face

There is a statement, regularly used in the educational literature and in conversation, that for effective school leaders, 'It is all about performance'. This is a delightfully ambiguous statement! Performance means both achievement *and* putting on an act. Many student teachers are told in training and by mentors that the art of teaching lies in performing and it is just as true of leadership. Performing is acting and the truth, therefore, about those apparently very assured headteachers is very different. The longer you remain in headship and the more you work and talk with headteachers of all ages backgrounds and degrees of experience, the more you realise that much of the role involves an act, actual bluffing and presenting a face to meet the particular situation or occasion in which you find yourself.

The importance of being yourself

In Chapter 4 I explore in some depth the importance of being yourself – accepting who you are, recognising your strengths and weaknesses and finding the leadership style that works for you. Wanting to be a head is of course very different from possessing the basic skill-set required if you are to stand any real chance of doing the job well. If you are certain that you want to have the opportunity to run you own school you will need to be able to do some things easily and well. In my view, for example, you will need to be able to:

- read people and situations accurately (most of the time at least!)
- recognise and acknowledge mistakes quickly, and learn from them
- deal assertively and incisively with a wide range of issues – often in rapid succession
- switch relatively effortlessly from one topic/issue/problem to another
- relish multi-tasking
- write easily and persuasively
- talk convincingly and with conviction
- sift through paperwork quickly and have the courage to put rubbish in the bin
- be a sponge – an instinctively intuitive sponge
- utilise sophisticated levels of emotional intelligence
- spot ideas and take risks which are likely to change things for the better

- sleep well even after a really tough day
- maintain a healthy work/life balance
- acquire a thick skin as and when the need arises because on occasions unpopularity comes with the role.

This list is not intended to be exhaustive and it would be foolish to maintain that anyone considering headship should possess all these skills in their entirety. There is, however, no doubt that if, for example, you are not someone who instinctively reads situations well, if you have difficulty expressing yourself, if you can only think of one thing at a time or if you are naturally cautious and conventional, it is going to be significantly more difficult to do the job effectively. Some people are just not cut out for the job because they do not have the essential skills and temperament best suited to it.

There is no doubt that confidence and knowledge inevitably increase the longer you are doing the job and learning quickly from mistakes is a pre-requisite; however, that being said, all headteachers will tell you that they have their fears, some of which grow the longer they are in post, their black and blind spots and that they will always find some demands of the role incredibly testing. You may, for instance, be surprised to know that the two aspects of the job that many of the heads interviewed found increasingly difficult were taking assemblies and managing governors (a challenge which will be explored in a little more detail in Chapter 6). Other challenges that never get any easier are dealing with difficult staff and effectively handling totally unreasonable and confrontational parents.

Conclusion

I hope that this chapter has gone some way to pointing out the possible pitfalls and the reasons why so many people either never get round to applying for the job or find it so difficult to find the right combination of events and circumstances to allow them to be offered the chance to run their own schools. However, I am in no doubt that headship is the most exciting, challenging and inspiring job in education with its enormous responsibilities and tremendous opportunities to change things for the better. Although the pace, variety and complexities of the role are daunting, the rewards are huge if you get it right and I would encourage anyone seriously considering taking on a headship to do all in their power to make the aspiration a reality.

Action points

- Don't spend all your time waiting for the perfect job. It rarely, if ever, exists. Accept any and all interviews: they will help you develop your technique and provide you with invaluable on the job training.

- If you manage to get an interview, do absolutely everything you can to make sure that you do your best. Don't be intimidated by the opposition. Remember that a lot of headship is putting on a performance and this is just as true at interviews as it is in any other aspect of the role.

- Many governing bodies assume that they are going to appoint the finished article to their particular school. They won't, so make sure you gain their confidence and support by creating a positive and constructive working relationship with them and with the Chair of Governors in particular.

- Find a mentor – someone whose character, confidentiality and guidance you can trust and someone who will tell you the truth – even when it is not what you necessarily want to hear.

- Access the best professional development opportunities available and tap in to as many useful and informed sources of help and advice as you can. Remember that a great deal of headship is learnt on the job so learn quickly and efficiently. Accept that you will make mistakes, particularly in the first six months to a year, but do everything possible to avoid repeating them. Keep a log/diary for future reference.

4 Finding your own leadership style

The impact of life history on leadership style

Research into what makes for effective and transformational leadership will often make reference to different leadership styles (strategic, learning-centred, emotional, entrepreneurial, ethical, political, distributed, sustainable etc). No doubt you could add to the list. All of these interpretations of how a leader operates are of course sensible, logical and reasonable and, if you think about it, it is relatively straightforward to work out what makes each of these leadership styles different and powerful. Far more difficult is to assess which if any of these approaches suit your style of leadership and what makes you instinctively use any or all of them when you are doing the job day after day.

In 2000 – seven years into my first headship – I was very fortunate to be given a six-month sabbatical by the governors of the school at Leicester University and the National College for School Leadership (as it was then known) as a part time lecturer on the MBA programme and a research associate. I absolutely loved the time out! The professor of my university department was an acknowledged expert on the impact of life history on school leaders and his enthusiasm and expertise convinced me to undertake some research of my own into the topic. As a consequence, I elected to interview five heads who had taken on and transformed schools in very challenging contexts.

The research (largely qualitative) centred on extensive interviews over two weeks lasting six hours each in total, with each of the heads where the areas covered meant asking lots of questions about their personal lives, their fears and apprehensions, their triumphs and disasters, their guiding mentors, important events and people in their lives and why and how they did what they did. It says a lot about these heads that when I called them out of the blue to suggest prying to this level into their own lives they all agreed immediately and enthusiastically to take part. They also said that at the end of the interview process they had all really benefited from the experience because it had, for the first time in their lives, given them the opportunity to talk about themselves and re-analyse why they were the heads they were. One of them memorably described the experience as rather like an extended version of Desert Island Discs – without the music!

Passion and intuition

The research dissertation I completed for the National College was titled 'Passion and Intuition' (Parker, 2002) and it is, I believe, still available on the National College website for anyone who may be interested. I make no apology for referring to it extensively in this chapter because it centres on a long-cherished view I have held, namely that although there is plenty of evidence to support the assertion that key aspects of leadership can be learnt, how you act and behave as a leader is largely dependent on who you are as a person. Much of what we do as leaders comes from who we are as people, which in turn is a by-product of what we have done and who and what have been major influences in our lives.

Starratt (1996) emphasised that we work as we live and have lived and how we react to situations will be coloured by our personal history, by our cultural roots, by our class, gender, ethnicity etc. Bennis and Nanus (1985) also noted that the point was not to become a leader but to become oneself, to use your skills, gifts and energies in order to make your vision manifest. It was important to withhold nothing but instead become the person you started out to be and to enjoy the process of becoming.

Talking heads

Sue, the head of a medium-sized inner-city primary school believes three people shaped and defined her leadership style:

My father was an enormous influence. From as young as I can remember I always had this overwhelming desire to please. I was the only daughter and my father was a very successful businessman. He always felt that it was important that I 'kept up' and the effect of those two words, which seemed to imply constant potential criticism that I wasn't 'keeping up' made me feel slightly inadequate – all the time! I think, on reflection, that he thought that because I was a girl I was not going to be able to take over the business when he retired and he was desperate to keep it in the family. He was old-fashioned in his outlook and would never have understood how much his fears, borne out of a common prejudice in those days that 'women don't do that sort of thing', did nothing for my self-confidence.

Although my teachers told me I was bright, I walked out of my A levels because I thought I was going to fail them. I still find it difficult to believe that I managed to become a head! The other two people who influenced me were headteachers I worked for in my formative years. The first one was a very old-fashioned paternalistic man who couldn't cope with new initiatives, government directives or any administrative tasks. He was happiest doing design and technology in his overalls with the kids who loved him. I was never sure what he did other than read *The Racing Post* avidly every day. But he had the quality to make you want to please him and always managed to make everyone working with him feel special.

The second head, a woman, was from the modern school of leadership, was always rushing around with a stack of files under her arm. She spent a great deal of her time out of school attending what she considered to be high-powered meetings, knew none of the staff and few of the children and produced a huge number of written documents which she put up on the staff noticeboard. Things kept changing on a whim and none of us had a clue what her central strategy was or what we were supposed to be doing. It was utter chaos. Both these heads in their different ways, one positive and one negative, taught me the importance of motivating people and making sure they knew what we were trying to achieve.

Finding your own leadership style

Five highly-effective headteachers

Defining characteristics

My research for the 'Passion and Intuition' paper centered round five very successful, very different headteachers who had all earned well deserved reputations for making significant and enduring improvements to their respective schools. All of the five heads were very different in terms of approach and personality:

- All of them ran their own manifestly successful schools in very different ways.
- None of them fitted into the generally accepted, established model that supposedly makes for an effective and dynamic headteacher.
- None of them had seriously considered teaching before embarking on their career which, by their own admission, they rather drifted into.
- Three of them never really enjoyed their own education very much; the other two went to local grammar schools and loved their time there.
- In spite of this, they admitted that they did not achieve academic results that in any way reflected their innate ability – this in spite of their parents' desire that they should do everything they could to succeed at school.

Three came from working class backgrounds, two were from middle-class backgrounds and all five had stable, loving and secure family upbringings. Four of them attributed their relative lack of academic success at secondary school on their own school experiences, claiming that they were never really inspired at school to develop a love of learning for its own sake – a memory that fostered in all of them a determination to do as much as possible to ensure that the children at their own schools were given every opportunity to excel and be actively involved in what one of them described as 'quality learning'.

Although they had some things in common in their backgrounds they were very different people in their own right, and yet their defining philosophies and practices were remarkably similar. For example, they had no time for posturing and pomposity and always judged people much more on what they did and who they were as characters and much less on what they said or claimed to have achieved. One of the heads put this down to the fact that his father had spent much of his adult life in the RAF and had as a result, somewhat surprisingly, developed a healthy disregard for hierarchy and perceived, received status. Another had come from a tough working class background and had had to endure the scoffs and taunts from so called 'posh boys' at the local grammar school where he had managed to secure a scholarship. Both of these early experiences had instilled in them a dislike of self-promotion and a determination to avoid any prejudice when it came, for instance, to appointing staff.

None of them had any overriding ambition to be headteachers and yet all secured promotions early on in their careers which meant that they were all deputy heads by the time they were in their early thirties. They each attributed their rapid rise to senior leadership positions to having a very low boredom thresholds and a real tangible fear of becoming stale. They also had sufficient confidence to believe in their ability to make a difference. They arrived at headship more by accident than design but all of them loved the job from the outset and relished the opportunities headship gave them to introduce innovations and pursue initiatives that advocated and promoted excellence. One of the most interesting findings from this research was the degree to which all of these heads had similar drivers when it came to leading their respective schools.

Passion for learning

All five heads used the word 'passion' when they were talking about the staff and students in their respective schools and all of them traced that passion back to their upbringing. One of the heads – a gifted sportsman – talked of the influence his father had had on him in this regard. Although by no means a naturally talented sportsman, his father loved competition and he had an iron determination to do whatever it took to be as good as he could be at any sport he took on. His particular love was football and although not especially gifted, his father prided himself on being known as a fearsome defender who rarely let opposing players beat him. He never gave up and always put 100 per cent into every game he played. He saw his father's passion when he was playing sport and music and how much it meant to him. He learnt from him that to be half-hearted and lukewarm about his own ambitions and the ambitions of those close to him was unacceptable. It had been a clear guiding principle for the whole of his working life.

This passion did not come from a training manual. It was not learnt or acquired when they began teaching. Rather, I noted, it came from their life experiences:

> Their determination to secure the best life chances for their students and the reason in the end that they all entered teaching did not spring from some intellectual exercise that convinced them that education per se was worthwhile. It came instead from a realisation that their good fortune in having a stable

family environment where the importance of education was acknowledged and promoted should never be taken for granted.

(Parker, 2002, pp.32–3)

Many young people have no such good fortune or solid grounding and these heads were very aware that for many of the students in their charge what happened to them during the school day would have a direct influence, positive or negative, on their attitudes and aspirations for the future. 'I know,' said one of my interviewees for this book,

> that most of my kids have a pretty loveless, joyless, pointless (in their view) uninspiring time for about 80 per cent of their week. I've got to do everything humanly possible to make the other 20 per cent as inspiring and challenging as possible if they are to have any chance of success when they leave school.

Their passion, therefore, came from doing whatever it took to make sure that atmosphere and culture in their schools actively encouraged their students to set themselves the highest possible aspirations and be constantly and consistently encouraged to do so.

Maverick leadership

All of these five heads were unabashed mavericks. This did not mean that they were reckless or unprofessional but they were natural problem-solvers rather than problem-creators and for this reason they frequently looked at means and methods that did not necessarily follow local authority protocol or what other heads regarded as 'official perceived wisdom'. One of them told me that he would challenge any and all so-called 'sacred cows' or supposed 'no go areas' if they got in the way of securing a better deal for his students.

They were gifted and entrepreneurial fundraisers who were always looking at ways to get money into their schools to improve the quality of the infrastructure and hence the quality of the learning. One of the heads loved the fact that he had managed to get famous people – Brian Conley, Nick Gillingham, Betty Boothroyd and Steve Redgrave – to present prizes at his speech days. No one thought he would be able to tempt such A-List celebrities to such an unfashionable school in a run-down suburb of Birmingham, but seeing the look of disbelief on the students' faces when these people walked into the school made all the bargaining and persuasion worthwhile.

Competitiveness

Just as their life histories had instilled in them a passion for learning, those same life histories also had made them all extremely competitive. The head who was a gifted sportsman told me how he utterly hated coming second and that even if he was playing a game of beach cricket he was determined to win. Another of the heads was a single mum and felt that part of her drive came from a deep-seated desire to compensate for the fact that her own daughter did not have a father in her life. I am not for one minute saying that competitiveness is a pre-requisite for headship but, for these heads, being competitive was a natural component of their leadership style.

All of them mentioned frequently during their interviews how powerful their parents' influence had been in creating this keen competitive edge and how much their respective life histories had developed in them a keen desire not to come second:

> All five heads traced their competitiveness back to their roots. Their parents wanted them to do well and spent their formative years encouraging them to have ambitious targets and fulfil their potential. They must have played a part in producing five school leaders who have proved throughout their careers that they are winners. These leaders' careers have without doubt been instrumental in teaching them how to win but it is their life histories which have been instrumental in shaping their intense desire not to lose.
>
> (Parker, 2002 p.34)

Defining moments

All of these heads paid tribute to influential mentors who had guided them through their early professional lives and were guiding them still. They also talked of defining moments in their lives which, on reflection, had fundamentally influenced their own leadership style. One head mentioned a serious boating accident that put him in hospital for a long time:

> It really shook my confidence and made me realise that I was not indestructible. I felt beforehand that I could control my own destiny but this episode caused me to change my outlook. Now I am calmer because I know things like this can come along which are outside my control. I'm more philosophical about things now.
>
> (Parker, 2002 p.18)

A second head remembered the following incident that had happened to him at secondary school:

> I ended up in the B form probably because I was the only boy in the new entry from the local council estate. On the second day I was told in class to pick up my books – in front of everyone – and walk into the other class, the A form. It was public, awful and humiliating. It was a hugely formative moment in my life not least because of the ridicule I received from the other children for being the focal point of such a public spectacle.
>
> (Parker, 2002 p.20)

A third head mentioned an uncle who came over from Jamaica to train to be a vicar. He made her re-think her own racial identity and convinced her that she would be bested suited working in schools with a strong multi-ethnic culture and a clear philosophy centred on tolerance and inclusion.

Another believed that passing the entrance exam to a highly selective grammar school encouraged him to pursue an academic career – the first member of his family to go to university, in fact. Yet another felt that marrying early and surviving a very tough few years of having children when there was hardly enough money to keep mouths fed regularly, shaped his attitude and approach to subsequent leadership roles he took on. He became far less judgemental and much more sympathetic to staff and students who were finding it difficult to cope.

All I can do here is capture a flavour of the pedagogical and philosophical values held by these remarkable headteachers. For me, what is especially significant is the extent to which they saw themselves as perfectly ordinary: hard working certainly and driven by a determination to do best by the schools they were responsible for but they would be the last people on earth to describe themselves as 'superheads'. The lengthy discussions I had with them reinforced in their own minds that they owed much of their success, drive and determination to factors that had initially been largely outside their control, namely their upbringing, the people who deeply influenced them and the events and circumstances that had such a profound influence on how they approached their jobs. As one of them put it:

> The excellence agenda I advocate very much comes from my life history experiences. I'm a workaholic – totally driven. I always have to do everything to the best I can. I started running and ended up doing marathons. I have done some stupid, extreme things but I can't help myself – it's just the way I am.

Leaders: born, not made?

It might initially appear that leaders are produced by a particular set of circumstances dominated by their own lives. Put simply, it could be argued that if you as an individual did not have instilled in you, virtually from birth, essential leadership characteristics, then you will never have the necessary abilities and aptitudes to take on a senior leadership position. This, of course, is not the case and there is plenty of evidence to support the view that people can become much better and more effective leaders by accessing high-quality leadership training, working with experienced and successful leadership mentors and by reading the right literature!

However, the research evidence to date on the impact of life history on leadership style (of which, as I have already mentioned, there is relatively little) would support the view that leaders are born first and made second. I have met many people in my career – and so I am sure have you – who you know with absolute certainty that however much they tried to develop leadership skills or however much training or advice they sought, they would never be able to carry out a senior leadership role successfully or earn the respect of those people in their charge. As people they just do not have what it takes – and that, I am increasingly convinced, will be the result more than anything else, of their own particular life experiences.

Talking heads

Graham, a long serving and extremely successful headteacher of a large inner-city primary school in the West Midlands told me of a deputy head he worked with for many years who tried unsuccessfully for much of his career to secure a headship:

> To be honest he wasn't a very good deputy head. He had fallen into the position almost by accident by virtue of the solid dependable long service he had put in at the school and the fact that he was appointed to the role by a governing body who I think took pity on him. Harsh, but true.
>
> I remember one incident in particular with great clarity. We had both gone for lunch together in the school canteen and I had a short but quite amusing conversation with one of the dinner ladies. It was the sort of exchange I had with staff every day of the week. We chatted for a couple of minutes, exchanged pleasantries and I must have said something faintly amusing because I left her giggling!
>
> When I joined him at the table he asked me what I had been talking about. I told him quite honestly that I couldn't remember much of the detail. I had just done what came very naturally to me – made contact with a member of staff and left her, I hope, feeling good about herself and about the work she was doing. It was something I probably did about 50 times a day and considered to be a vital part of my role in maintaining the feel-good atmosphere that was such an important part of the school's culture.
>
> He said, with some regret, that he just couldn't do that sort of thing because 'he didn't do small talk'. That one sentence for me encapsulated why he had never and would never achieve his ultimate ambition to become a head: he had neither the personality nor the necessary understanding of what the role demands ever to be able to do it effectively. It just wasn't in his make-up.

If I had to come down on one side or the other of the 'leaders born not made' argument I would argue that leaders are born first, made second. They can acquire new skills and knowledge but their values and attributes will be deeply engrained and non-negotiable. I also believe that you have to possess certain key qualities to be a good head – emotional intelligence is one pre-requisite for example – but those skills can be widened and honed by learning more about the role and how other people manage to do it well. Dimmock and O'Donoghue (1997) argue that it is important that individuals' current state of knowledge, skills and attitudes, as well as the significant and the relevant events in their life histories and past experiences, be acknowledged as key filters and lenses through which the meaning of best practice and principles are distilled.

I have already made reference in Chapter 2 that only one in 20 of the teaching workforce in the UK manages to secure the top job in school. Gronn and Ribbins (1996) explore the causal factors linking biography, leadership and careers and argue that a clear understanding of life history can lead to a greater understanding of leadership and what factors propel that five per cent of the teaching contingent into headship. They consider the possibility that effective, dynamic leaders share common attributes and that organisations screen their leadership cohorts in any way to guarantee conformity to preferred cultural types or models.

From this they suggest that there is something significant in the life histories of educational leaders that makes them far more likely to reach the top of their profession and enjoy the experience. However, they are quick to acknowledge that the field of leadership studies has remarkably few benchmarks or parameters for examining the circumstances of leaders' lives in relation to one another and also in respect of the culture and societies from which they emerge. (ibid)

If life history plays a crucial part in developing the skill-set and moral compass for preparing people to take on leadership roles, then there is every possibility that what happens in the highly-formative episodes and events in people's lives will be extremely significant in determining why some people and not others aspire to leadership. West-Burnham (2002) echoes this view when he says that it is in the essence of what it means to be a person that the foundations of leadership are to be found, and that it is impossible to conceptualise leadership without a model of the essential components of an effective person.

No one would argue that there is a pre-determined life history blueprint that will guarantee that one person will secure a headship and another will not. There are, for example, many different events, social contexts and experiences that will develop in any individual a sense of competitiveness, a clearly defined work ethic or a passion for achieving the highest standards. However, what happens in your life will help define how you will approach headship, so be aware that critical moments and important mentors will greatly influence your leadership style.

Talking heads

James, the head of a selective mixed grammar in the south of England, reflected on what made him apply for headships:

Everything prepares you for headship even some of the trivial things that happen to you. That's your educational food! I had a relatively privileged background but went to a dreadful school. I think wanting to be a head came from a combination of not having had a good experience at school and suffering university politics, where the main order of the day was school and teacher bashing. I know these things made me want to be a good teacher. However, the defining moment for me was when I started to study for a doctorate in philosophy and for some reason the head of the school I was working at asked me to write a mission statement and a rationale for what our school was 'fundamentally about' (his words).

What struck me with considerable force was the huge irony of all this because this particular head was not only quite incapable of delivering any part of the mission statement but was, at the same time blithely ignorant of the fact. No one had any respect for him or his so-called principles but he was blissfully unaware of the trail of educational carnage he left in his wake. Working with him helped me define in my own mind how I wanted to do the job. If I had to describe my leadership style I'd say it's constantly anchored in the principles I believe in combined with a sort of petulance that everything must be geared to student outcomes. My main strength is that I will do whatever it takes to see something through to a conclusion. A major weakness, which I am working on, is reacting too quickly to snippets of information. I also worry all the time about whether I've really got hold of the full picture where my school in concerned.

Know your strengths, acknowledge your weaknesses

A common misconception held by teachers and observers is that headteachers by definition do not believe they have any weaknesses. Good leaders will not allow false modesty to get in the way of identifying and making best use of their strengths and if you look at the vast majority of adverts for headships you cannot help but be left with the impression that only superhuman people with no weaknesses at all can or should apply. The list of qualities appears to be endless, with the ability to inspire everyone around them, manage transformational change effortlessly, communicate superbly and have an up-to-date, encyclopaedic knowledge of every educational initiative over the last 20 years taken as read. It is no wonder that many potential candidates are deterred from applying after reading such a daunting list of essential requirements.

Acknowledging your weaknesses

The reality is very different: headteachers all have many strengths but they also have many more apprehensions and weaknesses than they would care to admit in public. My interviewees were happy to share some of their own weaknesses with me. For example:

- I worry too much. I remember thinking for a long time that I was too 'fluffy' (i.e. too soft and approachable)! I also spend a lot of time thinking I am going to fail.
- I am extremely stubborn. Sometimes I will not be advised no matter what. I also work ridiculously hard and get bogged down in detail too often.
- I don't like conflict and get bored far too easily if there isn't anything exciting on the agenda.
- I am quite vulnerable to knocks and setbacks. I wish I had a thicker skin.
- I talk too much and interrupt people. I hear myself sometimes and have to make a real effort to shut up. I also want everything done yesterday.
- I find any sort of bereavement among staff or students incredibly difficult to deal with. I always feel I end up saying the wrong thing.
- I'm terrible at networking. My friends tell me it is absolutely essential but I just don't seem to be able to get the hang of it.
- I'm too volatile. Sometimes I convince myself that I actually like having a row.
- Far too often I stick resolutely to snap decisions. I know it's wrong on some occasions but I can't help myself.

Accepting your weaknesses

Like several of my interviewees I have always lacked confidence – something I believe I can trace back to early childhood. My parents were both from working class stock and my mother had been in domestic service as a junior housemaid for several years before she married my father. My father stayed in the same electro-plating firm for the whole of his working life, which turned out to be 62 years – joining the firm when he was 16 and finally retiring at 78! I was always taught to 'respect my elders and my betters' and my 'betters' invariably seemed to live in bigger houses than us, drive expensive cars and speak differently! I am certain that is where my instinctive feelings of being inferior come from. If I ever went for an interview, as soon as I met the other candidates I would be intimidated if I felt they had a more expensive suit on or 'looked posh'. As a result I was always incredibly surprised if and when I was appointed to a post – a feeling greatly intensified when applying for headships.

Accepting your weaknesses is not easy, of course, requiring as it does self-knowledge set alongside the ability to be constructively self critical about what you know you can do well, what you see as real blind spots and what you can improve on. It is possible, sensibly and realistically, to allow your weaknesses in one area to become strengths in others. For example, my lack of self-confidence has meant that I am certain I never allowed myself to become arrogant (even if others would disagree!) because I was always convinced that if I started parading my strengths or supposed achievements I would immediately fall flat on my face.

In my experience the best teachers and senior leaders I have worked with have tended to doubt the ability they have, that all around them see and applaud and maybe that is why: they never take anything for granted and are always looking at ways in which they can improve their performance. Another positive consequence of lacking confidence is that you tend to beat yourself up when things do not go to plan, much more harshly than anyone else does and this makes you more determined not to repeat the mistake in the future.

Addressing your weaknesses

No head will be brilliant at all aspects of headship and it is important to recognise and compensate for those weaknesses by introducing strategies that overcome them. I have never really been interested in, or thoroughly understood, financial budgeting, this in spite of the fact that in my second headship the school's annual budget expenditure was close to £14 million. I have also found analysing data accurately both difficult and, if I am honest, rather tedious – as is detailed work on health and safety. However, I am well aware how important these areas of work are when leading and managing a school.

Appointing the right people to the right posts

The solution is of course to compensate for your weakness or relative indifference by appointing people to these tasks who are exceptionally good at it and who you can trust to handle that degree of responsibility. That way you can keep an overall view on what is happening but not be troubled by detail that will in all probability go straight over your head. This is in no way suggesting that you should adopt a casual or laissez-faire approach to these crucially important factors in maintaining standards but you need to clarify in your mind exactly what you need to know and then make sure that you are kept informed.

A first-class premises manager, if he or she is any good, will sort out any and all health and safety matters. As far as the budget is concerned, you need a slightly anal, extremely organised and preferably experienced business manager or bursar who will, for instance, keep you informed about the percentage year on year spent on staffing and capital expenditure and whether funding to subject areas is meeting staff expectations and keeping in line with inflation. You will also need to know whether there is any possibility that you will be facing difficult times in terms of budget any time soon and, if that is the case, that there are robust contingency plans in place.

As for data, you need in particular to be clear that the targets that are being set are clear, widely disseminated, challenging and achievable, that individual faculty and whole-school targets are well-known to staff and students and that the trend is pretty much in line with predictions. But you do not need to get bogged down in detail unless you are really keen to do so. It is all too easy for heads to become surrogate business managers or IT managers or data systems managers and in the end that does not help anyone, least of all you because that is not the best use of your time or your attention. By micro-managing in this way (a fatally easy trap to fall into) you are in fact turning a potential leadership strength into a real weakness and disempowering those very people who have been appointed to help empower your leadership.

The importance of being yourself

Another feature of my leadership style was an in-built need not to trade on the status of the headteacher role and never to take myself too seriously. My parents had always quite naturally taught me to respect authority but they afforded people with titles or 'important jobs' an automatic degree of respect and subservience, which on occasions I felt bordered on the absurd. For example, doctors could never be wrong, lawyers and accountants were god-like and anyone carrying out a senior managerial role was treated like royalty! The effect of all this on me was to regard anything which smacked of status-seeking with deep suspicion and I was determined when I first took on a senior leadership role that I would not use or abuse the status that came with the position.

This fear of parading status came to an unexpected head when I was appointed to my first headship post. As a deputy head I had always enjoyed not taking myself too seriously and had acquired quite a reputation for telling appallingly weak jokes – to staff as well as students. My headteacher told me that it was imperative when I became a head that I introduced a little more gravitas into my style of leadership. He had always asked people to call him by his surname and even now I find it difficult to use his Christian name when we meet! He felt it was important that when I started at my new school the staff I made sure the staff called me Mr Parker. I decided to accept and act on his advice.

In the summer holidays before I took up post, quite a number of things were making me feel uneasy about taking on the huge responsibilities of headship not least whether or not I would be any good at it. However, the thing that caused me as much concern as anything was coming to terms with a situation where I would from now on be known, not as 'Richard' but as 'Mr Parker'. The thought of it felt alien to me but I was determined to run with it because I knew that my ex-boss invariably gave very good advice and he was utterly convinced that it was the right thing to do.

On my first day, after the first, immensely daunting talk to staff I attended a year meeting where I was to be the senior link. Halfway through the meeting, a member of the design department stopped proceedings and with exaggerated courtesy said: 'Headmaster, (never 'headteacher' or 'principal' for him!) how would you wish that we address you from now on?' This of course was the perfect opportunity to put my plan in action. I opened my mouth with the clear intention of saying 'I would prefer it if you all call me 'Mr Parker' but instead, to my horror, what I heard myself saying was 'Anything you like as long as it's not Rat Face…'

Driving home that evening I berated myself for being such a fool and for saying something so monumentally stupid but my wife gave me the opportunity to re-visit what I had said and why. She told me that deep down I was never going to like being called 'Mr Parker' because it just did not sit right with me. 'You've never given the formal trappings of status any credibility before so why try to start creating status now? It would never have worked. It was right for your boss but wrong for you. You are just not made that way'.

As ever, she proved to be a perceptive sounding board. The 'Rat Face Response' (as it became known) was the real me and I realised a very simple but nonetheless vitally important lesson about leadership. You have to be yourself (even if that means, paradoxically, putting on a performance from time to time) and you have to be true to yourself. The advice I had been given was excellent advice for some people – it just was not the right approach for me. Ten years later when I left the school, one of the farewell cards I received from the staff had written inside: 'Good luck with your next job. It's been nice working with you, Rat Face…' I cannot begin to tell you how much that meant to me.

Pause for thought

- When you are 'preparing a face' to meet a particular person or situation, remember it is a face and not the real you; being true to yourself is vitally important.
- The most important part of leadership in my view is to understand and maintain the personal integrity that makes you what you are.
- If you try to be someone else in order to please other people you will fail to gain the confidence of your staff and not fulfil your potential.

Be the leader you are, not the leader you think you should be

You need, in the final analysis, to find a style of leadership that suits you. There is a real temptation to assume that in order to be a head you have to be a particular sort of person and behave in a certain type of way. Your assessment of what you deem acceptable or unacceptable is very often heavily influenced by your memories of people who were in your view very successful, popular and effective leaders. Even though these people are not like you in any sense there is still the misguided urge to do whatever you can to be more like them and less like you!

And of course, for all the reasons I have been putting forward in this chapter, it will not work. You will end up presenting a pre-rehearsed face to your public that will be a combination of artificial gestures and characteristics of your guiding mentors that will leave you feeling unnatural and stilted. In the end, you have to find out what works for you and then stick to it. This does not mean that you will not learn certain tricks of the trade as you go along and change and modify some of the things you do as you become more experienced (I developed a much thicker skin, for example, after two years of headship) but underpinning everything must be an acknowledgement of what makes you tick, what you will and will not accept and why you decided to take on headship.

Talking heads

Elliot, the head previously mentioned whose deputies are not interested in headship (see Chapter 3) shared the following with me:

> A defining part of my teenage life was reading *The Grapes of Wrath* 12 times. My father was a tenant farmer who had a mental breakdown at 49 – brought on, I am sure, by the fact that his rent was put up year on year to an unmanageable level by a gentleman farmer who had, as far as I am concerned, no moral compass whatsoever but very expensive tastes.
>
> He spent a long time in psychiatric hospital. I won a scholarship to a direct grant boarding school where I was expelled in my A-level year having been caught by the housemaster one evening with a girl in my room. We were doing nothing more sinister than reading together but rules were rules. I lived in a tent on the Malvern Hills for the next three months and was allowed in school to take my exams. The head's wife cooked for me. I loathed the whole culture of the school, which was barren and oppressive.
>
> My father was a broken man from the moment he had his breakdown. A couple of years after his breakdown, the same gentleman farmer asked all his tenants to contribute to his son's twenty-first birthday present. I sent him a rotting fish head in a kitty cat tin. Looking back I realise now how these events really shaped me in that they made me see things from the point of view of those who are less powerful. I think my real strengths are that I get on with people whatever their rank or social background and earn the respect of the kids because they know I don't pre-judge them. My early life experiences I am convinced have made me much more naturally empathetic and I am grateful for that.

Conclusion

There is ample opportunity to develop your knowledge by attending the right training and accessing the best advice. I have always thought that if headteachers new in post had compulsory high-quality training in the following areas, for example, many heads would start their jobs much better prepared:

- the recruitment of staff
- health and safety matters
- financial budgeting
- effective performance review procedures
- dealing with trades unions
- campus development.

There are some European countries where all newly appointed heads have a month's residential preparation prior to taking up post which seems eminently sensible to me. If leadership is divided up into knowledge, values, skills and attributes, then knowledge and skills can be learnt but values and attributes will be part of a leader's make up and part of his/her life history.

It was interesting to note during my interviews how animated all the headteachers who contributed to this book became when the discussion turned to their own lives and the extent to which their backgrounds defined their approach to their working lives. There is no doubt that the best school leaders reflect on who they are as people and work within those parameters and restraints, accepting that in certain things they will always act in a particular manner because that is who they are. Of course experience will make you a better leader and the most effective headteachers learn rapidly and constructively from their mistakes. It is however, ultimately your responsibility to reflect long and hard about what makes you who you are and how that will affect your own particular leadership style.

Action points

- If you accept the fact that life history will determine much of your own leadership style, take the time to build up a personal profile about what you consider to be your defining values and attributes.
- At the same time compile an honest list of your strengths, apprehensions and weaknesses and how best you can manage all three.
- The more you trace your own family history and the impact it has had on how you as an individual do things, the more you will understand why you are as you are – and be comfortable with that. Remember the defining moments!
- Take time out to talk to fellow senior leaders about their own life histories. It is illuminating and very worthwhile personal and professional development – for both parties.

5 Keeping up to speed

Chapter overview

This chapter will examine the following areas:

- How to manage all the information and initiatives that come your way.
- How to develop the knack of knowing what you need to know.
- Using your leadership style to keep abreast of developments.
- Knowing where the channels of information are and how to access them.
- Developing and maintaining relationships with key players and exercising effective quality control.
- How and when to use (the right) mentors.

The challenge

Any conversation you have with an experienced headteacher, one recently in post or even those who are aspiring to the position sooner or later will turn to this topic. As a relatively experienced deputy headteacher working with a boss who seemed to know everything, I remember thinking that one of the reasons I could never be as good a head as him was because I had neither the skill nor, if I am absolutely honest, the desire to be as encyclopaedically knowledgeable as he so evidently was. This fear of not knowing is a common one – particularly among less-experienced heads.

Judith's observations on the next page are telling and very relevant when it comes to keeping up to speed, because so much of being a head is to do with balancing priorities and accepting the inevitable reality that there are only 24 hours in the day and that information overload is a constant threat to how well and effectively you do the day job.

Talking heads

Judith, a long serving head of a successful and well-regarded large comprehensive in the south west of England remembers her early days in headship:

> I will never forget going to my first county-wide headteachers' conference. I was, if I'm honest, pretty apprehensive anyway but when I got in the room I straightaway felt completely out of my depth. Everyone who was there appeared to be so comfortable in the role and, even more alarming, seemed to know everything. I was introduced to the chair of the conference, a long-serving, highly-regarded fellow head, who was so at ease with her surroundings that she made my own sense of inadequacy even more marked. During the pre-conference tea/coffee refreshments, I elected to keep my counsel and as far as possible keep my mouth firmly closed.
>
> When the meeting finally got started, my fears were re-doubled: during the many opportunities my colleagues had to contribute to the items on the agenda, they frequently referred to local/regional/government initiatives or policy decisions that I had never heard of. I had no idea how they managed to stay so effortlessly up to date and manage the day job at the same time. Of course, now, with the tremendous benefit of hindsight, I realise that many of the frequent contributors to these debates were as knowledgeable as they were because they spent far too much time keeping up to speed and parading their knowledge at these meetings and far too little time in their respective schools doing the job they were being paid for. I also found out in subsequent conversations with fellow heads that they were feeling as overwhelmed as I was. That was such a relief!

Managing everything that comes across your desk

The key here is the word 'managing' and not 'dealing with' the vast amount of information that headteachers have to sift through day by day, week by week. Of course, everybody is different and all leaders will develop a strategy that works for them. Some of the heads interviewed for this book have said that they have a reading pile and set aside time each day to look through it. Other heads leave the majority of the reading matter to the weekend to deal with it. Others still are much more cavalier and only really look at things that interest them. There is no one way that is better than another but the important thing is to develop a strategy that allows you to keep your own particular head above water and avoid that feeling of inadequacy that Judith talked about earlier. How you do that will depend very much on your own personality.

Talking heads

Mike, a long serving, recently retired headteacher of a large mixed comprehensive in the south east of England described how he kept up to speed:

I read the Times Educational Supplement every week without fail. I also got in to the habit of 'applying' for jobs because I found out really useful titbits of information from their paperwork about how other schools operated. I made a point of attending lots of conferences throughout my career. Even if the content of the conference was of no value, the coffee/lunchtime chats invariably were. I kept a box where I put every piece of paper that came across my desk that didn't require an immediate response. At half term I put the box in the back of the car and took it home. At the end of term I ditched it. I felt that if I hadn't returned to whatever documentation was in there by then it wasn't important.

I found that the longer I did the job the more I relied on instinct to decide what to run with and what to discard. At the forefront of my thinking were the needs of my school (particularly if it was addressing known weaknesses) and what the next 12 to 18 months were going to bring in terms of new ideas and initiatives. I always tried as hard as I could to be ahead of the game – or at least abreast of it! It is important to have people round you who will take the initiative, people who can discuss ideas with you as equals. And it is just as important to create the culture where you are not expected to know everything and come up with the ideas. As soon as you and/or your staff slip into that state of mind, you are lost.

Some leaders are naturally inquisitive about any and every new proposal or government initiative and will want to know as much as they can about everything even though they may only use a very small amount of the information they accrue. Others are only interested in what they believe to be specifically relevant to their own agenda and will discard everything else. Some people are extremely business-like about how they keep up to date (witness the head who sets aside allotted time slots each day) but other heads have the courage, and some might say foolishness, to be anything but methodical and worry far less about what they do not know. The trick is to have strategies in place that ensure that you avoid that feeling of being overwhelmed by everything that comes at you; easy to say of course but vitally important just the same.

Talking heads

Anne, the headteacher of a highly regarded 11–16 academy in the north east of England, told us how she manages to keep abreast of things:

> I am fortunate in being a very quick reader. That aside, I have very efficient systems in place. And I get rid of things quickly. Every day I go online and check the local news, the BBC, National College and Times Ed websites. I also have ASCL (her teaching union) briefing papers.
>
> Because I know my school very well now and feel confident that I am up to speed with what my staff and students may or may not need to know or consider, I am fairly ruthless when it comes to taking on or ignoring information that gets on to my desk. That being said I accept and welcome any and all suggestions from colleagues who may have read something that they think may be of interest. I think that is very important.

Knowing what you need to know

Up to this point I have been concentrating primarily on the written word: books, websites, publications, educational pamphlets, briefing documents, email etc. However, keeping up to speed involves much more than 'reading stuff'. Peter, the head of a large 11–18 academy in the North Midlands, made the following observation when he was asked how he managed to keep up to date:

> I rely very heavily on instinct when it comes to knowing what I need to know. Whether that's a good thing or not, it's how I cope. I think you need to know what

works for you and for your organisation and that is rooted in your values and in your passion for learning.

I think that is incredibly important.

David Jackson, who went from the headship of a large, nationally-acclaimed school in Bedfordshire to director of the Network Learning Group at the National College for School Leadership, echoed a similar sentiment in an early keynote speech he gave to headteachers shortly after the National College opened for business. An important theme running through this keynote was his questioning of the apparent need for headteachers to have a clear vision of where the school needs to go and that this view is communicated lucidly, consistently and persuasively to their staff and students. He argued that it was, in his view, rather presumptuous of any school leader to assume that he or she has gone to the top of the mountain, looked out and captured exactly what is going to make his/her school exceptionally successful and effective for the foreseeable future.

He said that it had never been like that for him. Looking back over his career he realised that he had always rejected school development plans largely as a waste of time and had, more often than not, lurched and stumbled his way through each phase, frequently arriving at a destination that was new, exciting and surprising, that had never been in his mind at the outset as an articulated and closely planned objective. This used to bother him early on because he worried about the fact that chaos rather than order was driving his headship and the school's development. He came to realise however, that the school's direction and culture were dominated by its values and its attributes.

He arrived at the conclusion that he knew instinctively what would work and what would not work for his school because he understood what made it tick. That knowledge was priceless because it meant that when policies or initiatives came across his desk or when he was at meetings where ideas were being promoted, he knew which ones to back and which ones not to touch. The chaos he referred to was still key to the school's development but that chaos was directed by a set of values, philosophies and pedagogies that made it all work. 'You don't always know which horses are going to come racing down the track but more often than not you will know which ones to back, was how he put it. And it makes sense to me.

Sense or nonsense?

This will not, of course, make sense to everyone. Some headteachers will probably be appalled at what appears to be a rather haphazard and cavalier approach to school leadership/development. They will need clear development plans, they will need lots of widely-disseminated documentation which shows clearly and unequivocally where the school is at present and where it is heading in the mid/long term. And there is absolutely nothing wrong with that, but it is vital that you find an approach that works for you when it comes to keeping up to speed. If you only feel comfortable when you think you know exactly what is going on in your school all the time then you will have to find strategies that help you manage that need.

The only word of warning I would give is that adopting such an approach is almost certainly going to put huge additional strains and pressures on your time and energies. It is important to bear in mind that all of our interviewees – without exception – said that they are comfortable with the fact that keeping up to speed does not mean knowing everything. It brings to mind the words of a chief executive of a major American corporation who said that he found that if he went ahead with 75 per cent or more of the facts he never usually regretted it. The guys, he said, who want to have everything perfect drive you crazy! It is an important consideration to bear in mind.

If you interview an experienced headteacher who enjoys the respect and admiration of those with whom he or she works, almost without exception, they will tell you they have an acute sense of when their school is operating well and when it is not. They will be able to walk around the school and pick up very quickly on the mood and atmosphere of the place.

Talking heads

Stuart, the head of a very large primary school on the south coast was once asked to describe his role and responsibilities. He made the following analogy:

> I've loved sailing for as long as I can remember and it is still the one thing I do that takes me away from my job and allows me to think. The boat I have at present I helped build and I have been sailing it for well over 20 years. I feel I know every screw, every piece of timber and every last inch of sail cloth as well as I know my wife and family!

> When I am sailing I know instinctively if the various squeaks and creaks are good or bad, if the sails are at full stretch or not and if the various instruments are working accurately. The trick is to set the boat up perfectly to make sure that you are getting as much speed from the wind as possible. This means

making sure that you have the boat sailing in exactly the right direction and that the sails are angled in to the wind at the precise angle and depth to make the best advantage of the weather conditions, whatever they may be.

This is very much like headship. Your job is to keep the school moving as smoothly and efficiently as it can in the right direction. You have to know your own school as well as you possibly can, have a clear picture of where you're trying to get to and then use all the various internal and external influences to help you move in the right direction as quickly and effectively as possible.

If you are in tune with your school you know it inside and out. That doesn't mean to say that you are up to speed with every single detail of what is going on but you have a clearly defined working relationship with it which comes from a combination of explicit and implicit knowledge of what makes it tick. You know when the creaks and squeaks are acceptable and when they are highlighting a problem. It's a kind of sixth sense.

Quite often, this sixth sense that Stuart talks about can be judged against known facts. If, for example, a headteacher walks around a faculty or subject area a couple of times in a week and just feels that the working atmosphere is not right, it is relatively straightforward to match these implicit reactions with explicit data to check if all is on track. If it is not, it is important to act quickly and decisively and if constructive criticism is needed, it is equally important to work with the relevant staff to put in place strategies to improve things. Senior leaders must avoid criticising their colleagues without expecting to do anything explicit to help or providing any moral support if, for whatever reason, they are struggling to cope.

Pause for thought

- Remember that no matter how convincing some headteachers may be in persuading you that they know everything, they do not! Take time to work out what you need by way of information to stay afloat.
- Do not be over-influenced by other headteachers who appear to know

and need to know so much more than you. Do your own thing and be guided by people whose opinions you trust.

- If you attempt to keep properly up to speed by reading everything that comes across your desk (most of which will carry an 'important' tag with it) you will do little else.

Quality control: creating channels of communication

Leadership style and school culture

There are many channels of communication available for a head to access in order to keep up to speed with what is going on in their school and maintain a clear perspective on how the school is doing – in its widest possible sense. The extent to which you as a head are successful in tapping into these rich veins of information very much depends on the culture of the school (i.e. whether it is 'open' or 'closed') and the ethos (i.e. how far it is centred on trust or suspicion, high or low blame etc.), which in turn very much depends on how you are as a leader.

In the broadest terms, at one end of the spectrum leaders can be centralist in leadership philosophy, distant and unapproachable in manner and lacking whatever it takes to trust the people who work for them. At the other end of the spectrum, leaders can be open, approachable and confident in the ability of those working alongside them to have the energy, commitment and talent to deliver if and when they are given the opportunity and the responsibility to do so. Autocratic leaders are much less likely to create the right circumstances to allow a free two-way flow of information. Leaders who micro-manage are also less likely to encourage the people around them to be open and truthful. Leaders who worry about their own status will create a climate of fear and apprehension where the expectations are high with the tendency to blame people for under-performing or making mistakes and where the unwritten rule among staff is not to express a view or argue a case.

Therefore, the type of leader you are will have a major impact on the extent to which you can develop and maintain the many and various channels of commu-nication which will give you priceless indicators about your school's state of health. I believe that the more open and democratic you are as a leader and the greater the sense of openness and constructive accountability that exists in your school, the more likely you are to keep up to date with what is happening, to be given confirmation when initiatives are well received and to be given the 'heads up' when things are not as they should be.

Leaders who are by nature autocratic and uncommunicative will, in all probability, not be able to access the wide range of information streams. Goldstein (1998, p.116) commented that 'the tendency of top management to isolate itself from the front troops is fatal'. Leaders who are naturally distributive in style are also much more likely to be given information on a regular basis. Those headteachers who, as I have already mentioned, practise high expectations/low blame among their colleagues and who genuinely delegate roles and responsibilities are much more likely to receive honest and constructive feedback. Leaders who operate an easy to reach, open door policy (although the door will still need to remain firmly closed when the occasion demands) are much more likely to foster the positive relationships with staff and students that encourage open dialogue and honest exchange of views.

This is so important: headteachers can easily fall into the trap of spending too much time in their offices, with the door closed, pouring over data and minutes of meetings, lesson plans, faculty reports or emails etc. so much so that they rarely get out into the school, walk around and get that sense of well-being – or otherwise – that can tell you so much more about the state of the school than any report could. Elliot, one of our interviewees, told us about what happened when an extremely IT literate headteacher started at a medium sized tough working class inner-city comprehensive. Prior to his arrival at the school a daily briefing was held when all the staff came together for a few minutes to hear and give messages, present any immediate concerns etc. – and to have a chat! He had emailed Elliot to say that he was delighted that early on in his tenure he had replaced the daily briefing with a fairly sophisticated IT system which meant that there was no longer any need for the staff to meet together every day. Instead, they were all required to log on to their laptops to find out what was happening.

Elliot emailed back to say that he thought that was a huge mistake. The daily briefings were, as far as he was concerned, incredibly important because they gave the staff the opportunity to meet formally and informally and the amount of knowledge/information that can be picked up during these few minutes was invaluable. It was also important, in a big school, to have this personal contact each day – it was a sort of daily health check. And the social benefits were tremendous. Elliot's concerns were taken on board by this new headteacher and the daily briefings were re-instated.

Developing and maintaining key relationships

I have already mentioned the importance of getting the balance right between keeping yourself away from people to have time to assess information and to catch up on relevant documentation and being with people to seek out their views and listen to their individual stories. In my experience, the heads who know the most and enjoy the greatest confidence among their colleagues and students are those who rely less on the written evidence and much more on the spoken word. They believe much more readily what people tell them face to face rather than what they write in memos or reports and create the context in which everyone at the school is encouraged to express views and challenge what they consider to be ill-advised ideas and/or innovations.

A recurrent theme running through this book is the extent to which headship is a people-centred activity. As school leaders, you will spend much of your time interacting with a wide range of 'clients' all of whom will bring different issues, problems and challenges for you to deal with. A headteacher I worked for some 20 years ago used to say to me that he 'didn't do any work at work' anymore. At the time (a relatively young, still pretty raw deputy headteacher) I did not really understand what he meant. With the priceless benefit of hindsight I know now exactly what he meant. As an approachable and easily accessible school leader, his office door was rarely closed, always occupied by two or more people and when he was not there he could be seen walking the school and talking to teachers, students, caretakers, visitors – anyone in fact who had any sort of contribution to make to the school's development. This meant that time at his desk doing paperwork, responding to letters (this was pre email!), reading important documentation, making phone calls was either done at the very end of his working day or at home. I cannot remember seeing him sitting at his desk working although he obviously did but not, as he said, when he was 'at work'.

I mention this because I have not met anyone since who was so knowledgeable about his school. Nothing seemed to escape him. If I ever had some information to hand on, he invariably already knew about it already and I can think of no single occasion when he was taken by surprise by something that happened at school. At one meeting I remember him talking about the views of the silent majority as being key to the school's success or failure. The trick, he said, was to make sure that the leadership culture ensured that the majority did not in fact remain silent!

By accessing the views of all the interested stakeholders and by making sure that the leadership team at the school kept their doors, eyes and ears open, the chances of important information being lost or misinterpreted were greatly reduced. It is important to consider how leaders can make sure that they keep the dialogue open with as many people as possible and create and sustain effective working partnerships with all the key players.

Pause for thought

- Leadership, as I have already stressed elsewhere in this book, is a people-centred activity and if you think about it, that means spending much more time with people and much less time with paper!
- All of the interviewees said that the longer they are in the job, the better they become at avoiding information overload. New heads take note.
- Be aware that if you maintain healthy and mutually productive working relationships with the people who will tell you the truth, you will be much more likely to keep abreast of what is really going on in your school.
- Don't assume that those closest to you will always necessarily tell you the truth. More often, they will tell you what they think you want to hear.

The information gatherers and sharers

The head's PA or secretary

Surprisingly little is written in any books on headship about the role and importance of the head's private secretary or PA as they are often called. I have known headteachers who have been driven to distraction by having to work with poor and inefficient secretaries. Those same heads' working lives have been transformed when they have managed to rid themselves of a weak PA and replace them with a brilliant one. I was extremely fortunate to have excellent secretaries throughout my headship. They were all different in the way they worked, all very different in personality, but each one had the four essential ingredients that I believe every good PA needs:

- complete confidentiality
- the ability to be an honest and sympathetic sounding board where you can express views and frustrations in a way impossible with any other member of staff
- an unerringly keen ear to the ground for picking up information and 'vibes' and knowing instinctively what you need and do not need to know

- to be organised, efficient, accurate and mistake-averse.

Quite simply, they can make your job a great deal easier to cope with and the best become virtually indispensable.

Rosemary Litawski, writing about her third headship in *Headship Matters* (2002, p.13) honestly describes how much she was indebted to her own secretaries:

> The working relationship with your personal secretary is a vital ingredient not only for the smooth running of the school but, possibly even more importantly, the headteacher's state of mind. A key characteristic must be their discretion because they witness my moments of elation, my frustration, my lapses of memory and energy, my moments of despair, my loneliness – and even my tears. I have trusted them with my secrets – professional and personal. Just having someone to talk to who is the soul of discretion is worth its weight in gold.
>
> My secretary is my gatekeeper, my filter, knowing when to turn away photo-copier salesmen and when not to put a press reporter through. Her strengths probably reflect my own failings, my own unpreparedness. I was unprepared for my loss of autonomy, with such simple things as someone 'keeping my diary', 'arranging my appointments' – in other words, managing my time.

Experienced school leaders will echo and identify with these sentiments. In addition, a good PA will be invaluable in helping you keep up to speed. She (and yes, it is *almost* always 'she'!) will probably know more than anyone else on the staff, apart from you, about what is happening at the school and what is coming over the horizon. Most PAs will be at all leadership and governors' meetings and will also be the one person who talks to just about everybody around the school, using the PA as a quick way of getting information through to the head. The filtering role Rosemary talks about is very important: too much information is just as bad as too little. A good PA will get that balance right much more often than not.

The leadership team

The one group who are pivotal to how well you as a head keep up with what is going on is your leadership team. The important thing to bear in mind is the extent to which this team will be effective in this regard depends on two factors: your working relationship with them and their working relationship with the staff and students. Get either or both of those wrong and the extent to which you will be able to keep up to speed will be severely curtailed. If you are moody, inconsistent, prone to outbursts of rage and frustration and publicly dismissive of any ideas or information that are suggested by others, you will not only be an immensely ineffective and unpopular leader, you will also never be given any help in taking on and sifting the vast quantities of information that comes with the role.

Instead, you need to be approachable (that word again!), open to ideas, sympathetic to constructive criticism from your senior leadership team in particular (not easy at all), slow to anger, quick to praise. You also have to be prepared to admit that you do not know everything and that new information is always welcomed and acted upon. Keeping your door open as much as possible helps enormously because your leadership team will often want just a couple of minutes with you to pass on some information or to share an idea and they do not want to have go through the whole process of making an appointment and preparing a paper in order to do so. That will almost always put people off from coming to you again.

That culture of openness and approachability with the staff needs to be embraced by your leadership team. If they are always in meetings or locked in their offices 'doing work' and are 'far too busy to be disturbed', they will not become those receivers and filters of information which make such a difference to the extent to which you as head can keep up with what is going on. They need to accessible, they need to be sympathetic and they need to be honest. They also need to be seen to get things done and take on board concerns or criticisms which will often be made to them but never to the head.

A popular, well respected deputy head is a priceless asset in this regard. The best ones I worked with had superb working relationships with staff and as a result found out vast amounts about what was going on – good and bad. They never went in to the staffroom or the canteen or the library without their antennae on full alert and even though the coffee and idle break-time conversation appeared innocent and non invasive, they always managed to pick up things of value. This does not mean that they operated as sort kind of headteacher's mole! Far from it: they were liked, known to get things done and only unhappy when people were not fulfilled and energised by the work they were being asked to do.

Teachers

In most schools there will be formal procedures for making sure that people are kept up to date with what is happening in school. Many schools have daily briefings, websites, newsletters, school intranets/VLEs/email systems which will allow the free flow of information. There will also be regular staff meetings, subject manager/head of department/year/faculty gatherings, subject/learning reviews, lesson observations, school assemblies and briefing notes. It is really important that all these vehicles for keeping up to speed are kept in good working order and that what is said is factual and productive.

Many heads will have annual meetings with all staff as part of a performance review programme. This is obviously easier in a smaller school but even in larger ones, there are heads who put aside a sizeable amount of time to conduct one-to-one interviews with all staff in order to gauge how things are and discuss the needs of individual staff. It is very important to back up all these eminently sensible and worthwhile activities with informal structures and practices which enable people to meet with you on other occasions. It could be in a corridor or at lunchtime or when you are on duty or having tea in the staffroom (many heads do go into the staffroom, some do not). Being accessible is the key. There is no point, for example, going to great lengths to have fixed formal interviews with all staff if you are locked away in your office, unavailable, for the rest of the time.

Students

It seems ludicrously self-evident to say that in order to keep up to speed with what is going on in your school and how well you are doing, it is a good idea to seek out the views of your major clients – the students – regularly and systemati-cally. Effective leaders and good schools do this all the time but headteachers can create a sense of sham consultation/responsibility among their students so that the general feeling among the student body is that their views are not really important and their contribution to the school's development not properly valued. It is incredibly important to avoid making this mistake. Students, if treated with respect and trust by you and the staff, will give you a great deal back in terms of constructive feedback and valuable insights.

Again, as with teachers, senior leaders can and will use formal and informal structures to keep up to speed with what is going well and not so well. Effective practice might well include:

- regular meetings with groups of students to look at their work and elicit their views
- work shadowing students
- school council meetings
- students involved in learning observations
- spot checks of students' files
- one-to-one interviews

- lunchtime meetings with the headteacher
- exit interviews with students leaving the school
- regular feedback questionnaires
- teacher/student learning surgeries etc.

No doubt you could add many more of your own. All these practices have their place and can provide valuable information streams that will give you honest feedback and suggestions for future innovations or improvements. However, as with teachers, there is no substitute for creating and maintaining an informal structure where students are encouraged to express their views and have their opinions treated with respect and welcomed as such. In my experience, the more you give young people the responsibility for assessing and looking to improve their own learning and the learning of others the more they will respond positively and maturely to the challenge.

One of the interviewees told me that if she really wanted to find out how things were in the school she went and 'had lunch with the kids'! If you are the sort of leader who finds it easy to communicate absolutely naturally with your students and are frequently out and about chatting to them, you will be astonished how much you learn and how quickly you pick up on the state – healthy or otherwise – of your school.

Other staff, other channels

Although teachers provide a rich source of information and opinions, there are many other sources that are equally revealing. Teaching assistants and cover supervisors, for example, spend vast amounts of time observing teachers and students in situ and can, if asked intelligently and sensitively, provide the leadership team with an ongoing assessment of how things are in the classroom. Caretaking staff are equally valuable in that they can report incidents of out of classroom or school behaviour that can provide a valuable snapshot of the overall feel of the school.

I know of some schools where the premises staff are actively encouraged to become involved in the learning by carrying out pastoral duties and assisting in the classroom. This works well because more often than not the premises staff gain an additional insight into why teaching is such a demanding and sophisticated occupation and they realise that students who infuriate them by, for example, dropping litter or misbehaving in the lunch queue or the corridors can very often be very different when they are engaged in a learning activity that they enjoy.

The canteen staff and the cleaners can also be a rich source of information. Canteen staff tend to remain in their jobs for quite a long time and some of them will have seen the school go through many stages in its development. Clever questioning about the students' attitudes, their demeanour, even their eating habits, can be very revealing and give you an additional insight into the social and pastoral health of your organisation.

If you have managed to 'sell' the message of the importance of social capital and mutual respect to your students (and staff) the evidence of the success of that message will be much more telling and this is illustrated by the extent to which your students treat those with less overt status. Respecting teachers – experienced graduates who are knowledgeable authority figures – is one thing. Respecting others because that is what you do in an organisation that actively promotes mutual trust, respect and status is quite another.

Because schools are important centres in the local community, keeping up to speed inevitably requires regular engagement with local stakeholders. These can include the people living in the catchment area, local places of worship, councillors, shopkeepers, businessmen, youth or faith groups, charities, feeder schools, banks, supermarkets, bus companies etc. These people will give you extremely valuable additional information and perspectives about how your school is being rated by those who live nearby but do not necessarily have a vested interest in how it is performing academically. Of course, these opinions need to be tempered with a degree of caution. Close neighbours frequently have a fairly jaundiced view of your school because they see the students going into and leaving school – times when traditionally they are not always on their best behaviour. Bus companies can also have a partial view because again, students can be loud and, on occasions, thoughtless and inconsiderate when they are on public transport.

However, school leaders who maintain regular dialogue with all these interested parties are much more likely to benefit from so doing. Inviting local residents into school to see the students' work, attend school performances/ concerts and maybe have a tour is a sensible and positive thing to do. Having regular litter picks – by students – in neighbours' front gardens or volunteering to do errands for them also works wonders for community relations.

Mentors/fellow professionals

I have already talked about the value of having a mentor – someone you can trust and whose opinions you value. A good mentor can be a major asset when it comes to keeping up to speed and maintaining a clear view of how things are in your school. You don't have to limit yourself to just one mentor either. I found that throughout my time as a head I always had half a dozen or so headteacher friends who were at the end of a phone and who would fill me on details of new initiatives or government policy and, just as important, give me their steer on how they would respond.

Of course, you need to bear in mind that these friends will not always be in tune with the specific needs of your own school or any particular agenda you may be working to. That being said, as a litmus test on an initiative or an innovation you may be thinking of introducing or for providing a steer on some government policy declaration, they can be an invaluable help. They can also provide a calming voice of reason and restraint when your leadership team is doing quite the opposite!

Interestingly, the majority of the heads interviewed for this book had done additional degrees. Four of them had doctorates and the rest had masters' qualifications. All of them said that doing these second or third degree qualifications had been extremely demanding but had provided them with invaluable professional development and had helped them enormously in becoming more efficient and effective information gatherers and sifters. They had also made contacts and friendships with other students on the courses who had subsequently become valuable sources of information and advice.

Talking heads

Sue, a primary school headteacher, recently completed a PhD, an accomplishment she still gains much value and pleasure from:

> The research I had to do meant that I ended up interviewing 27 outstanding headteachers. Talking to these heads and being shown around their schools made me realise that a lot of my concerns were shared widely by other heads. It is odd how much you feel that your own particular fears, apprehensions and shortcomings are yours and yours alone but when you open up to fellow professionals, many feel exactly the same way!

> I absolutely loved and adored doing research. It gave me more confidence as a leader and I learnt so much. The networking with the other heads that came out of the research was extremely useful. I would recommend any senior leader to take on a major research project, I know it's challenging and time-consuming but you gain so much. It's invaluable.

Conclusion

This chapter has stressed the need for a constructive and healthy mix of formal and informal structures to help you keep in line with and even ahead of the game. It is such an important part of your role to be able to see the bigger picture, to sift the important from the trivial and to know which initiatives to run with and which ones to discard. Of course, you will have plenty of people around you to give you advice and guidance but one of the challenges of leadership is having the courage and perception to make the right call more often than not. One American president said that he had over 100 economic advisers to call on when he was making key decisions about the budget but when they provided him with over 100 different recommendations it was down to him to choose which one to adopt. No wonder: the buck stops with you!

There is no one proven way of keeping up to speed and auditing the quality of what you are doing but there is great wisdom expressed by those of our interviewees who said that more than anything else they looked for honesty and constructive feedback. Flattery and lip service have no place in an effective school. Many heads talked about their reliance on informal contacts, gut feeling and instinct to gauge how things are in the school:

- 'A lot of the information I pick up is informal – walking round the school, walking the corridors, talking to a whole range of people who will talk to you about their concerns, their achievements and their plans. You can learn so much this way.'

- 'A great deal of what I did was based on gut instinct. I would talk to senior staff if I was planning to do something but I found I had a sense of what would and would not work in my school.'

- 'I'm pretty ruthless about what comes across my desk but the longer you do the job the more you just seem to know what is worthwhile and what is not. I certainly don't read anywhere near as much stuff as I did early on in my headship.'

- 'It's difficult when you are a new head. It's very easy to feel totally overwhelmed by the amount of information that comes racing at you from all directions. I find now that I do much more talking than reading and expend my energies concentrating on the things that I think will benefit my school. The rest I largely ignore.'

- 'I realised after a while that you had to believe in certain key principles and allow them to guide what you got involved in and what you didn't. I never jumped on a bandwagon simply because it was a bandwagon.'

- 'I have always read a lot and am fairly disciplined in the way I keep up to date with what is happening locally, regionally and nationally. However, I find that my thinking is more and more driven by instinct now – knowing what works for you. I know that that instinct is driven by my core values and my passion for learning.'

The anecdotal evidence gathered from the headteacher interviews suggests that there is no proven way to keep up to speed and maintain a clear view of whether your school is setting and maintaining the highest possible standards of teaching and learning. The secret is to find what works for you as soon as possible and then stick to it.

Action points

- Find people in your school, and outside it, whose opinions and judgements you can trust and use them as sounding boards.
- Try to come up with simple, effective ways of keeping pace with everything. Having you and your leadership team, for example, set and review tasks and targets for each term is a straightforward way of keeping up to speed – and of maintaining corporate accountability!
- Learn to sift the good information streams from the bad and then be fairly ruthless about how much time you give the latter. Avoid the sense that you are drowning in paperwork by being disciplined and consistent in adopting strategies that keep you afloat.
- Never complete a questionnaire, fill in some feedback form or answer a phone call from an educational agency unless you are absolutely sure that it is going to benefit the students.
- If you have never considered doing a further degree/qualification, think again. The evidence from those heads who have done so is overwhelmingly positive.
- If you do not have a network of trusted mentors and friends, try to find one as soon as possible. You will not regret it and in the long term it will save your energy and reduce your angst.

6 Coping with internal and external demands

Chapter overview

This chapter will consider the following:

- The challenge of managing governors effectively and constructively.
- Getting the right balance between being in and out of the school and maintaining the right partnerships.
- Dealing sensitively with local, regional, national, international interactions/ invitations.
- Handling the media.
- Dealing with time wasters, flatterers, local stakeholders, salesmen, consultants, dignitaries, local residents.

Managing governors effectively

In this chapter it is really only possible to scratch the surface of what is a complex and demanding working relationship between school governors and the headteacher. Dealing with governors effectively requires great skill and diplomacy from all concerned parties. How this relationship begins and grows is dominated by the personality and attitude of individual heads and the extent to which they can build and sustain constructive working partnerships with their governing body and most especially their respective chairs of governors. However, it is difficult to set down firm guidelines or rules of engagement where this relationship is concerned because what works for one head and his or her chair of governors will in all likelihood be anathema to another – and vice versa.

The unique challenges

There are few areas of school leadership that highlight the contrast between reality and rhetoric than the role, place and importance of governors. Governors are capable of causing headteachers considerable concern, stress, angst and frustration. Union officials are quite open about the number of heads who contact them in tears over issues to do with governors and dealing with governors frequently appears high up on the list of things in headship that cause most soul searching and upset. Alan, head of a large secondary school in the Midlands, admitted that he found governors a real trial:

> It's a weakness of mine – I know it is. I just do not have the patience. If I'm honest I find governors in the main to be an immense trial – they're like an albatross round my neck. The fact the school I inherited had just failed its Ofsted inspection made it a hundred times worse. Thank goodness I've always been blessed with a strong chair of governors.

This is not to say that every head has major problems with governors. Many heads will quite rightly pay tribute to the commitment and loyalty of their governing bodies and emphasise the place and importance of the role of the chair of governors in helping set the tone and direction of the school. However, how you manage your governors and how they in turn interpret their role and position in the school will be crucial in determining the extent to which you feel settled and fulfilled as a head.

Talking heads

Patrick, a very experienced long serving secondary school head remembers his first encounter with his governing body:

> It was 1993 and I had just been appointed to my first headship in a run-down medium-sized comprehensive school in Northamptonshire. The spirit in the school was very positive but the school buildings were in a terrible state and money was very tight. At that time the government launched the technology colleges' initiative where schools were invited to raise £100,000 of sponsorship, in return for which the government would match the funding and then award an annual grant which in our case would amount to well over £150,000 a year.

It seemed to me to be an ideal challenge to take on. The decision to seek technology college status and begin fundraising in order to become a technology college was taken at my first full governors' meeting. There appeared to be unanimous support for the idea. I was delighted and immediately set about trying to raise the money. A week later the chair of governors rang me and said he needed to speak to me as a matter of some urgency. It transpired that since the meeting a group of governors who had said nothing during the meeting were now concerned that the decision was the wrong one and had contacted the chair to say that we needed to call a halt to proceedings. I was so angry!

I pointed out to the chair that this topic had been fully debated and unanimously supported at the full governors meeting and any concerns or objections should have been voiced then. I also told him that if this was the way the governing body operated at this school I would have no option other than to resign. In view of the fact that I had only been in post for three weeks this was by any measure an extremely reckless thing to do and my wife was not at all happy! In the end it worked out very well. The governors backed down and my working relationship from that point on was excellent. We raised the money in four months and became one of the country's first technology colleges the following May, an event that helped transform the school over the next five years.

I am not advocating this dramatic response as a blueprint for how to work with governors but Patrick's account illustrates the importance of setting your own very clear ground rules about what is and what is not acceptable practice. After all, the reality is that the challenges facing headteachers and governors are considerable not least because the established blueprint laid down by central government is far from ideal. There are a number of reasons in my view for this. For example:

1 The rationale defining the role of the governing body is flawed. To have the view that the governing body operates in the same way as a board of directors in a major corporation does not work for two simple reasons: firstly, governors are not financially tied in to the organisation (they can for instance resign without notice and without any personal repercussions); secondly, the vast

majority are in effect well intentioned lay people who quite understandably cannot possibly have a clear and informed knowledge of how schools operate because such matters are inevitably outside their field of expertise.

2 Many governors arrive in post out of a sense of duty. Some choose to become governors because their own children are at the school and they want to get a clearer perspective on how the school operates. Others become governors out of a heightened sense of community service, which is obviously to be commended. They feel they want to make a personal contribution to the school in order to support the work of the staff and students. Some governors will be appointed by local authorities or by business concerns associated with the school. In all these examples, however, their lack of detailed knowledge makes it impossible for them to be instrumental in defining the major aims and objectives of the school in spite of what the rhetoric might claim.

3 Very often (and for perfectly good reasons) governors have neither the time nor the space to respond as quickly and efficiently as they need to on occasions in order to deal with the day-to-day business involved in running the school. PAs and secretaries will often comment on how difficult it is, for example, to call an unscheduled meeting of a governors' committee to address a sudden issue or emergency because all governors have their own commitments and calls on their time. Heads also tell me of the problems they have getting a group of governors together to help appoint staff – a reason why many governing bodies quite rightly and sensibly delegate that particular responsibility in large part to the headteacher.

4 The reality (once again) is that the model of governance the government has laid down assumes that a headteacher can expect the equivalent of a full-time commitment from governors to carry out their published responsibilities (which are huge) from people who can only ever be part time. Ironically, those governors who very often have the most to offer – local businessmen, accountants, lawyers, architects, builders, company directors, other headteachers, vicars, social workers etc. – are so busy in their own lives that by their own admission they cannot devote the amount of time to the role that the position requires if it is to be done properly.

Best friends? Worst enemies?

Having worked closely with governors for nearly half my working life, I believe that the best way to ensure that you establish and maintain effective and harmonious working practices with your governing body is (however bad it sounds) to be constantly aware that governors can, if you are not careful, be your worst enemies as well as your best friends. The degree to which they are one or the other depends on how you as the head manage them, but on occasions governors can be thoroughly unreasonable and put real pressures on the headteacher out of a misplaced assessment of their own roles and responsibilities.

Talking heads

Ann, the headteacher of a recently established 11–16 academy in South Yorkshire talked about her own particular issues with her governing body:

> I always try to be professional and am determined never to lose my temper. I don't let the governors get under my skin. I try to be firm but reasonable which is not always easy. To be honest the governors are a bit of a running sore at the moment and one of my key challenges. I do, fortunately, have a wonderful chair of governors. He comes in every week. He is a wise and perceptive sounding board and an excellent channel of communication. He is a thoroughly decent man.
>
> The problem is that on occasions you will encounter rogue governors and at the moment I have two governors who are being over-intrusive and demanding and creating an immense amount of work for me and my business manager. I wouldn't mind if it was of some value but the truth is it is a waste of time and does nothing to help me do my job more effectively. What governors forget to acknowledge is the distinction between governance and operational matters. As a result, problems arise and it is very difficult not to become irritated and defensive!

Governors govern and leaders lead

The mantra 'Governors govern and leaders lead' is one newly appointed heads would be wise to endorse. The best governing bodies accept the fact that they do not, and cannot, have a major role to play in the operational matters of the school. Governors who overstep the mark and try to become involved in day-to-day school business almost inevitably create more problems than they solve. Frequently, those governors have not understood that their major responsibility is to be a critical friend. One head I interviewed described this responsibility as 'providing the headteacher with a necessary cloak of accountability', which I believe is an interesting and perceptive way of understanding and acknowledging their primary role.

This does not mean that they give carte blanche to the head to do whatever he or she pleases. That would be irresponsible: they have the right to question and challenge practices and decisions where they think it appropriate and over-rule if they genuinely believe that the senior leadership of the school is pursuing a particular objective that they consider to be fundamentally wrong for the school. However, they do not have the right to become surrogate headteachers and try to do their jobs for them. After all, they have appointed this particular person to run the school and doubtless agreed a generous salary package to do just that.

Best friends

Governors become your best friends when they understand the limitations as well as the responsibilities of school governance. They will lend their expertise when it is needed, they will voice their honest concerns when they feel it is appropriate, they will give the head a constructively hard time if the arguments being put forward by the leadership team for a particular scheme or innovation do not seem to add up, and they will volunteer for activities that support the staff and students.

In the final analysis, however, they will back the headteacher if and when he or she feels passionately about an initiative that will improve the quality of teaching and learning in the school. And they will never presume to know more about running a school than the senior leadership team, demand excessive amounts of detail that they plainly do not need or interfere in areas of school business they do not need to know about.

I was very fortunate in my first headship to have two excellent but very different chairs of governors. My first chair was a director of a national production company and someone with an exceptionally heavy workload. He had no special relationship with the school but he had nonetheless a fierce loyalty to the place and was determined to do what he could to support me and the staff in making the school as good as it could be. He was intelligent, wise and enviably calm in times of crisis. In spite of his many commitments, he never missed a governors' meeting and was always on the end of a phone if I needed to talk to him and ask his advice. He was also quite prepared to tell me if he disagreed with something I was doing or thinking of introducing. Over the years he became a good friend and I still feel indebted to him for his wise counsel, his support and his unending ferocious pride in the school's achievements during his time as chair of governors. Our professional relationship worked so well because he knew when to get involved and when to stay back.

My second chair's personal profile could not have been more different. He worked with me for four years and was the first to admit that he did not really grasp the finer details of pedagogy or educational theory but nonetheless, he came to the school every Wednesday to help out in the school library and was a tremendous help, as a retired community policeman, talking to and counselling some of the more challenging and confrontational students. Furthermore, he knew many of the staff, attended every major school event and was clearly passionate about the school. But he never once assumed that he was there to do my job. Another priceless quality he had was humility. We were very fortunate at the time to have four technology college sponsor governors on the governing body – experienced, bright, articulate, entrepreneurial professionals who asked difficult questions, challenged constructively and perceptively and gladly gave of their time and expertise when they had the opportunity. The chair of governors realised the contribution these four governors could give to the school and he did everything he could to make sure they did!

Talking heads

Sheena, who runs an 11–16 academy in Hertfordshire, talked about the working relationship with her governors:

> I try to share as much as I can with my governors but it is important to give them the right information in the right format at the right time. It is also important to know what not to give them, too much information is just as problematical as too little.
>
> The bottom line is they trust me. Although I do not get a great deal of practical support and/or challenge I also get virtually no interference. The challenge for me is to keep them as informed as possible and make sure that we concentrate on the areas that will interest and engage them and leave the other areas for me and my senior staff to deal with. I feel that by so doing, the working relationship between the leadership team and the governing body is harmonious and productive – thank goodness!'

Getting the balance right

Sheena's assessment of how she works with her governors illustrates how crucial it is to get this area of your working life right by making sure that the way you work with your governors is as stress-free as possible for you and, just as important, for them. In order to maintain the correct balance there are some ground rules that you would do well to remember:

- Make it as clear and unequivocal from the outset what your parameters and expectations are regarding the nature of the working relationship between you and your governors.

- Establish a good, honest and open partnership with your chair of governors. If, for any reason you, as the head, are certain he or she is not the right person for you to do business with, do everything in your power to find another better, more suitable replacement.

- If, by any chance, you have governors who are pompous, pedantic and confrontational, do not lose your temper with them in public but do everything in your power to replace them or at the very least limit their negative influence on your school.

- Provide as much information as your governors need so that they can discharge their responsibilities effectively and make sure that all deadlines for governors' reports, papers etc are met.

- Be especially careful to ensure that all the school's financial dealings/ transactions are as transparent as possible and fully approved by the governors. That way you protect your own interests and your professional integrity as well as theirs.

- Make sure that you maintain an open door policy for governors. Avoid coming across as defensive at all costs. Welcome them into school and take advantage of any offers of help that are made by any and all governors.

- Having governors linked to subjects or year groups or particular specialisms in the school helps cement positive working relationships between the school and the governing body and shows that you are not trying to keep things from them.

- Wherever and whenever possible, recruit people onto the governing body who bring areas of expertise that you can tap into: architects, police officers, youth workers, councillors, lawyers, human resources managers, builders, and even other headteachers can be extremely useful! (One primary head told me that an architect on her governing body had in one year brought nearly £2,000,000 from the local authority into their capital projects budget!)

Getting what you deserve

One of my interviewees said that headteachers end up with the governors they deserve. This was said in a conversation where a headteacher was criticising headteachers who, in her opinion, gave far too much responsibility to governors and appeared to absolve themselves from most of the accountability that comes with the job. Although some governors can be difficult and obstructive on occasions, it is absolutely vital that you establish as soon as possible the conditions which will enable you and your governing body to work well together.

Pause for thought

- Remember that many governors give up their time freely and willingly and the vast majority are doing so for good reasons. Make sure that in your dealings with them you always acknowledge that fact.
- If you come across as hostile, aloof or distant with your governing body, you are going to create difficult and needless problems for yourself and for your governors. If you understand their priorities and they acknowledge yours, everyone is going to be more positive and upbeat.
- Remember that governors have an important role to play in running the school but make sure that the role is clearly defined and understood by all parties.
- Bear in mind that you will only end up with the governors you deserve by working hard to make sure that you end up with the governors you really do deserve!

Handling the media

The media, like governors, have to be managed sensitively and well. Managed well they can provide a consistent stream of positive publicity for your school that can be extremely valuable when it comes to events promoting your school. It is much more likely that the majority of your dealings will be with the local press or radio. Most high profile journalists and radio presenters cut their teeth working for local radio/newspapers and then move on to national papers, so more often than not the reporters who will be contacting you will be young, relatively new in post and keen to please their editors in order to advance their careers. You can help them and your school by giving them copy whenever they reasonably want it and even when they do not. On occasions they will contact you with some story that is potentially damaging for your school (drugs, scandals, poor exam results, problems with local residents, trouble on public transport, litter, anti-social behaviour by one or more of your students etc). The rule here is either to say nothing or to tell the truth. Make sure too that you do not allow your thoughts to be interpreted in the wrong way by clever journalists. As soon as they begin to say 'So, let me get this right, are you saying that…?' be on your guard! Whatever you do, do not try to cloud the issue or disguise the truth (do not lie, in other words) because nine times out ten, the press will find out the truth and your reputation will suffer as a result.

Try to avoid taking an unnecessary stand on any particular issue. I made a serious mistake one year by not giving the local press our school's examination results and not allowing them to come in to interview and photograph the students. At the time I believed that my reasons were sound: the interviews were superficial and invasive, the photographs tediously predictable (groups of students jumping in the air holding pieces of paper etc.) and the league tables designed only to put schools even more in competition with each other. The fall-out was significant among the parents in the town and in our catchment area in particular. The school had traditionally come top of the league tables every year and had again this particular year, but the assumption by everyone reading the papers was that we had had really bad results and were trying to hide the fact. So much for my principles!

The national media is another proposition entirely. I have spoken to heads who have been unlucky enough to have to deal with reporters who are following up stories that have been much bigger than the school. One head told me that following the tragic death of one of his students in a freak accident at the school, the journalists reporting on the event appeared to have no sense of context, proportion or any moral integrity whatsoever. They just wanted a story, they wanted interviews and would stop at virtually nothing to get them. At times like this, when you are under immense pressure to do the right thing and protect innocent victims from a media assault you must keep calm, take professional advice if you feel it necessary and never say more than you absolutely need to. At all times, provide a written statement and do not allow yourself to be quoted out of context. If the correct response at the time is 'no comment', stick to that, no matter what the temptation or the provocation.

Making the media work for you

There are numerous ways in which to ensure that you make the most of any media opportunities that come your way. If, for example, you have a major open evening coming up, making sure that you figure positively in the local media in the days leading up to the event can make all the difference. You can also get free publicity by so doing. Some schools use the internet to great effect in this regard. There are some brilliant advertising campaigns which involve the whole school and which project a powerful message about the inclusive and welcoming culture of the organisation. The local press and radio obviously use the internet to find stories and you can often get excellent follow up coverage to add to the weight of the original campaign. In this regard, it is vital to make sure your website is up-to-date, informative, attractive, modern and easy to navigate and make sure that your local papers have access to all your newsletters, sports reports etc.

Some schools appoint staff and students to be media ambassadors. They will make sure that any good news will get to the right people and they will also have a store of material to keep editors up to speed when, for example, there is a slow news day. Another very important consideration to bear in mind is the impact of social networking sites can have, thanks to the power of the worldwide web – it not only amplifies good news stories but will equally effectively spread the bad. One head of a high-profile independent school told me that one incident involving drugs that occurred in his school made national first or second story headlines in 246 countries within 24 hours of the story breaking. Remember, however, that in all these things, the fundamental rule here is that you should do whatever it takes to maintain the best possible relationships with the media or suffer the consequences!

Talking heads

Miriam, the head of a large multi-cultural primary school in south London shared the following story:

> One of my deputy heads, an extremely resourceful and creative teacher single-handedly set up a Saturday School (called Saturday Club) in our school for children and their parents. Within three months he had over 200 parents and children enrolled doing courses on cooking, trampolining, ICT, drama, golf, poetry reading, film making etc. It was a brilliant innovation and long before all the debate about full service extended schools.
>
> I wanted to get some national publicity for the project but nobody seemed interested. Then a major television company contacted me to say that they were making a programme on the issues surrounding bullying in schools and they needed a school background for the opening titles. They said they would pay us well for the time and inconvenience. I, unsurprisingly, initially declined the invitation. I was eventually persuaded for three reasons: the money was substantial and much needed, the producer assured me that any images of the school would be so hazy and faint nobody would be able to identify which school it was and most importantly, he promised to do a feature on Saturday Club in return for the favour and as a gesture of goodwill.
>
> They duly came into school and spent the morning filming in and around the school buildings and then left. The programme was aired two weeks later. To my horror I saw the opening shots that clearly showed the buildings and the name of the school with children running and playing in the playground. Then there was a close up of a child's hand followed by a large booted foot standing on it. The title then came on: 'Bullying in Schools: The Issues.'
>
> I was horrified and immediately contacted the producer who was extremely apologetic and said that he had been overruled by the programme editor. He said that he appreciated how angry I must be about what had happened but that he would try to help appease me by doing a really upbeat programme on Saturday Club. I never heard from him again. It was a salutary lesson and one that I will never forget.

In or out of school? Getting the balance right

As a headteacher, you need to be in school to do your job properly but on occasions you also need to be out of school in order to access the right information, support and guidance about issues that will affect your school. In some ways there is no right or wrong answer to when you should be out of school but in all probability, the simplest rule to observe is to be *in* far more than you are *out* and only go out if you are sure it is worth the time and effort. However, as with all simple rules, they are easier to preach than they are to practise.

Experienced heads have all commented on how difficult it is to gauge when an invitation to be out of school is worth accepting. I have been to conferences which were advertised as 'important' and 'not to be missed' only to discover that they were neither of these things. Equally, I have passed on invitations/events that have looked unpromising which turned out to be brilliant. There is no easy solution to this although as you become more experienced you will, as with training providers, gradually acquire a clearer understanding of what is worth attending and what is not.

A week into my first headship, I visited a neighbouring school which was highly regarded in the local community and run by an extremely popular and successful headteacher – someone who, over the years, was to become a trusted mentor and friend. During our conversation he gave me the following advice:

> There's no doubt that when you are appointed to your first headship it is an incredible exciting moment in your professional life. One of the things you will quickly discover, especially in the early days, is that everyone wants a piece of you and there will be endless opportunities to be out of school attending conferences, meeting fellow heads, having 'business lunches' with local dignitaries etc. Remember that the governors have appointed you to be head of their school and to do best by it. If you are out all the time you cannot be doing your job properly. Only take time out of school if you are absolutely certain the school will benefit as a consequence.

It was sound advice: over the years I have seen and met so many headteachers who have become high-profile local, regional and national personalities in their own right and discovered that their own schools have suffered quite dramatically the negative impact of not having the head in situ anywhere near enough. This does not mean that a school cannot function if the head is not physically in the school – that would mean that the leadership culture in the school was not strong, but a school cannot operate at its best if the head is frequently out of school and, inevitably, increasingly out of touch as a result.

The lure of regional, national and international networks

If you start to develop a reputation in the local and wider community as being a school leader with some influence it is likely that you will begin to receive invitations from high-profile organisations. I was six years into my first headship before the invitations started to arrive. Then, within three months I was on two regional steering groups, I was a member of the Specialist Schools and Technology Trust's Council and one of three heads to sit on the national steering committee. I was then invited to join a government think tank that was working up proposals to launch the Innovation Unit and the Leading Edge programme. I was also enrolled as an associate tutor with the University of Leicester to help them to deliver their master's degree in business administration.

There is absolutely no doubt that this sort of work is very exciting and seductive. You begin to get used to the idea of presenting papers in London venues with ornate curtains and chandeliers! You find yourself having meals in very nice restaurants and meeting with people who sit at the heart of government and who have real influence on education strategy and policy. A major advantage as far as your own school is concerned, is that you can raise its profile, find out sooner than other heads about real and anticipated government initiatives and put across your views to people who are genuinely interested in finding out at grass-root level what is happening in schools. I do not think that is a coincidence that in the three years I was doing this work, my school raised over £300,000 in private sponsorship and invited several guests, who ran major government departments, to visit the school and express their thanks and admiration for what they believed the school had achieved.

However, there are dangers in going down this route. I am sure the school suffered a little because of the number of times I was away from it. Any school (see Chapter 3 and Chapter 7) needs the regular physical presence of the head to maintain a sense of focus, stability and calm. Constantly being in so called 'high-profile' meetings and attending impressive but frankly showy events and dinners can make you feel somewhat short changed as a head when you return to what you may be beginning to see as the daily grind of running a school. As with so many other aspects of being a school leader the temptation to become involved in exciting activities or projects that will not significantly help or improve your school should be resisted by constantly acknowledging why you applied for the job in the first place. You cannot serve two masters!

Too much time out?

I know of headteachers who spend weeks on end away from school. For example, as the international implications of school leadership have grown more and more headteachers have taken advantage of opportunities to travel to other countries for extended periods. No one is saying that developing a global perspective is wrong; to do it once or twice is valuable and valid personal and professional development, but make it a regular feature of your headship and it will not be good for your own school.

However, is important for any head, on behalf of his or her school to maintain the right links with the right people for the right reasons. The best schools will have a wide range of local, regional, national and international partnerships and many of these partnerships will require the direct input and presence of the headteacher. Once again, you as a head will have to balance the demands of these external pressures and calls on your time with the day-to-day responsibilities of running a school. It is never easy! Interestingly, the evidence to date would suggest that although video-conferencing technology is now much more robust than it was, it is not anywhere nearly as widely used as it could or should be. This is surprising in view of how much it can and will help the development of international partnerships. No doubt the next generation of headteachers will use it much more extensively than the current one does.

Conversely, being in school every single day is not necessarily a good thing either. As long as you have the appropriate mechanisms in place to handle your absence (easier in larger schools of course) taking time out of school can be good for you and equally good for the school. No headteacher likes to admit it but all staff in all schools will occasionally like to have a day when the head is not around. That is in no way a criticism of the head.

Taking time out of school is also good for allowing you the opportunity and space to reflect and gain a different perspective on an issue or problem that may have been troubling you. Although I have mentioned elsewhere in this book that many training sessions do not live up to the hype, there is no substitute during these sessions for those tea/coffee/lunch conversations with fellow professionals that can often give you ideas and solutions that had not occurred to you. They also (see Chapter 5) help you keep up to date with what is happening locally and nationally.

Your decision!

There are, therefore, no right or wrong answers to this aspect of your working life. How you manage it is very much down to you as an individual. However, I hope the following thoughts may be of some use:

- Remember that the primary duty of care you have is to your own school. If you are out of school too much you will not be able to exercise that duty of care efficiently and well.

- If you can use video-conferencing etc. (particularly when it involves international partnerships) then you should do so.

- Make sure that any time you take off is properly planned and managed. Be certain that any lessons or scheduled meetings are covered.

- Learn quickly when and why you need to be out of school. When you are, make sure that on your return you get up to speed as quickly as possible and deal with any outstanding matters as soon as is practical.

- When you are out of school, do not spend all your time at the conference (or wherever it is!) contacting your school to check if everything is OK. I have always found it depressing to see the number of mobile phones that appear at every single conference break out session.

- Always make sure when you have been to a conference or another school or training session that you report back to the relevant people to let them know how the time out has been spent and how it has been of use.

- Occasionally and deliberately, engineer time out of school to give you time to reflect and plan ahead. You do need that space and freedom – and so does your school!

- Always treat time out of school as an opportunity to pick up or 'borrow' ideas which will improve practice in your school. The best heads I have met have been really efficient educational magpies in this regard – constantly on the lookout for anything that will be of interest or use in their own schools and quite prepared to use it in themselves.

- When you begin to find that time out of school is a welcome and necessary escape from the daily grind, take care and take note. This nearly always means that things are not right and need to be sorted out.

- Make sure that you keep a note of what training has been good and when it has been poor and try very hard not to waste time twice.

- Have the right support mechanisms in place, delegate sensibly and appropriately and then leave the people concerned to get on with it. Always assume no news is good news!

Dealing with different groups

I have already said that heads new in post frequently mention how many calls there are on their time to be out of school – often from people who do not bring much of value to the table. There are just as many requests from an often bewildering variety of sources to come into school and meet the headteacher and 'no one else will do'. At first it is hard to distinguish the genuine requests from the time wasters but most heads learn very quickly!

Andrew, one of our interviewees summed up a common approach employed by heads when he said:

> I never had any truck with so-called independent advisers or people who were clearly out to sell their wares irrespective of whether it was right or beneficial as far as my own school was concerned. My attitude to these time wasters was finely judged somewhere between direct and rude!

Regional and local authorities

For many heads a significant challenge has been maintaining constructive working relationships with their regional/local authorities. There are some excellent educational authorities in the UK who do sterling work with their schools but sadly there are many that do not. I have to confess that as someone who was the head of a grant-maintained, self-governing school for ten years, I have never had much time for local authorities and believe passionately that schools are much more effective when they are led and managed by heads and supported by enlightened governing bodies. I therefore welcome the recent political trend in the UK to free schools from local authorities and give them the opportunity to work with people and organisations that have the time and expertise to make a valid contribution to the improvement agenda.

At the time of writing there is considerable evidence to suggest that the power and influence of educational authorities in the last few years has much reduced. One of the reasons they have struggled to provide a relevant and worthwhile contribution to school improvement is because they have been given an overtly strategic role by central government when in reality they have only been able to carry out a commissioning role: many of these authorities have clearly not had the range and quality of expertise to do much more than deal with transactional matters and concentrate on trying to reverse the fortunes of schools in their charge that are deemed to be failing. Small schools that do not have the capacity to provide the training and support that larger schools can, will no doubt welcome the support of advisers and officers from the local authority but the signs are that the long established government model of delegating the responsibility for maintaining standards in our schools to third parties is fast disappearing.

That being said, it is highly unlikely (even if the UK government's flagship academy and free schools programme grows at the pace advocated by ministers) that heads will ever be given complete control over everything that happens in their schools. There are, after all, certain areas of work that most heads are delighted to delegate to third parties: school transport, school meals, legal advice and support, allocation of school places and parental appeals, certain landlord responsibilities, grounds maintenance, children who have been permanently excluded – all come to mind. It is likely therefore that headteachers will have to spend at least a small part of their day dealing with local officers who have commissioning roles to play in their schools.

The approach I have found to work has been to be professional at all times, to access any and all help and support from local authorities that has proved to be of value (many local authorities have, for example, very good personnel and capital project teams) and avoid any time wasters who inevitably appear on the horizon. In my view, the best aspect of self-governing schools is the freedom it gives heads to access the best training, the best expertise and support in all areas of school life without being restricted to one particular provider. That fact allows enabled school leaders alone to achieve best value for money so much more efficiently.

Jobsworths

If you are lucky enough to have a PA or a secretary who assesses situations quickly and perceptively and has the right level of initiative and judgement she will be a major asset when it comes to protecting you from time wasters and jobsworths. One primary school head told me that hers was not a 'jobsworth school' and her secretary felt just as strongly about people wasting her time as she did. As a result, it was very difficult to get past her secretary who became extremely proficient at deciding who would be given an appointment and who would not. By so doing she made the head's life a great deal easier.

Generally speaking, heads will delegate much of the work that involves dealing directly with suppliers, salesmen, advisers, trainers, local officials, bureaucrats etc. to other staff but this is of course much easier to do in larger schools. In a small primary school it is even more important to ensure that the people coming in to the school are providing relevant and worthwhile services and not wasting anybody's time. As one primary head said: 'I have a simple rule: if they've got something to give to the school, I'll give them my time; if they haven't, I won't.'

Talking heads

Brian, the head of a medium sized mixed 11–18 comprehensive in Devon, found the number of people trying to come into his school a real issue in the early years.

If I'm honest it probably took me about three years to work out how to avoid getting trapped in a room with someone who was doing nothing other than wasting time that I did not have to waste. I suppose, in retrospect, it was partly because I was naïve, too polite and slightly curious to see what they were trying to sell. I was fortunate in having a local authority link adviser who I got on really well with. She was especially helpful in pointing me in the direction of local authority personnel who were good and (in confidence) in warning me off those who were not up to the job.

In the end I devised a series of rules that worked for me and helped reduce my stress levels. I never answered anyone who was conducting a survey, I refused to discuss anything with a salesman or consultant before seeing something very specific in writing, I delegated any and everything that did not interest me directly and I allowed my PA pretty much a free rein when it came to fielding phone calls and deciding who would and who would not get an appointment to see me. The only people I would always find time for were fellow headteachers because they always brought something of interest and I almost invariably stole one or more of their ideas! The strategy that worked for me, I decided, was to be flexible, to get to know the people who were going to be your friends and then as far as possible stick with them – and be prepared to give them something in return.

Working with the local community

Up until fairly recently – certainly within the last 40 years – schools were allowed, even encouraged to exist in splendid isolation. Headteachers felt no need and had little or no pressure put on them to develop partnerships with the local community or engage with the wide range of local and regional stakeholders who have always had a vested interest in making sure that the educational standards in schools were as good as they could be. The situation has changed dramatically, in particular in the last 20 years.

Schools have opened their doors much more and they have put themselves at the centre of their communities. The Extended Services agenda in the UK which has encouraged schools to stay open longer, run after-school clubs and set up and run community initiatives is less strong than it was five years ago but the basic philosophy is still clear: schools need to operate at the heart of the community and as a consequence there will inevitably be calls on your time as headteacher to meet local dignitaries, attend functions and other events and welcome representatives from a wide variety of organisations, often on a rolling programme: local councillors, mayors, religious leaders, youth workers, sports co-ordinators will all be keen to establish and maintain working relationships with you.

Getting the balance right so as to make your own working life manageable (you do, after all have a big job already looking after your staff and students!) and not offend all these people requires high levels of tact, diplomacy and organisation. And all this crucially important work is hardly, if ever, covered on any headship training courses!

Pause for thought

- Deciding when to be in school and when to be out, or what to say or not say to the media are decisions that are fraught with potential danger not least because there are no right answers. In the end you just have to do what you think is right.
- However, as with just about everything else discussed in this book, you need to be confident that what you are doing is in the school's best interests.
- The issues being raised in this chapter illustrate how much a head has to be able to read situations and respond to them sensitively and well. Once again, the need for emotional intelligence is paramount.

Conclusion

This chapter illustrates the range and complexity of the relationships that impact on your role as a headteacher. I have mentioned elsewhere the degree to which headship requires you to play many roles, occasionally put on different faces and possess the skill to engage with so many people from so many different backgrounds all of whom have their own particular idiosyncrasies alongside their own specific agendas. Good communication skills, emotional intelligence (that quality again), excellent people skills as well as the ability to think rapidly on your feet and move seamlessly from one context or conversation to another are all tough calls (and pre-requisites) that you must be able to make if you are to manage this aspect of headship effectively and well.

As has been stressed throughout, although you may call on trusted colleagues to advise you how to manage your time in and out of school, the reality is that most staff will tell you what you want to hear. If, for example, you say to your leadership team that you are worried that you have been having too much time out of school they will disagree with you even though they may secretly believe that you have a point. Telling a headteacher that he or she is not spending enough time in school, even if you are a trusted deputy head, is very hard and the vast majority of people will duck the question. The solution therefore is firstly, to make sure at all times that you have a trusted mentor who will tell you the truth and secondly, to do whatever it takes to be honest to yourself and true to your principles and do what you think is right.

Action points

- In view of the fact that there are no right answers to so many of the issues raised in this chapter, keep a diary of how often you are out of school and a record of how useful that time has been to the school and to you personally.
- If possible, make sure that you or your PA/secretary keeps a file on what have been good or bad training experiences. If you go to a conference organised by a particular provider that is poor, it is highly unlikely that that particular provider will be any better in the future.
- Whatever else you do, build into your diary specific times for renewing contact with staff and students. That can mean, for example, making sure that at least once a week you spend at least half a day informally walking the school.

Apart from helping you keep up to speed with the whole school (see Chapter 5) it will keep you in contact with the most important aspect of your role – engaging with your staff and students.

- If the working relationship with your governing body is not as good as it could or should be, do whatever it takes to sort the problem out. Make sure that you have consistent procedures in place to set up and maintain effective working relationships with the media.

- Bearing in mind how potentially jaundiced and difficult local residents can be, keep up a consistent dialogue with them. Listen and respond constructively to their complaints and wherever possible do some community service for them. Litter picking, shopping trips, invitations in to school to design exhibitions, carol concerts, school plays, occasional lunches etc. can improve the working atmosphere dramatically.

- If you are convinced that taking time out of school for a specific purpose is worthwhile and of benefit to you and your school do not be deflected by apparent criticism from staff. Stick to your principles.

7 How to keep the school buzzing

Chapter overview

This chapter addresses the following:

- Why this is one of the most important aspects of the senior leader's role.
- The importance of treating people as people.
- How to motivate staff and students.
- The importance of being around and being seen.
- Dealing with/sidelining destructive influences.
- How to keep upbeat and positive by creating the right atmosphere.

The headteacher effect

Without exception, the interviewees who have contributed to this book have cited the challenge of keeping the school moving with purpose and positive intent as the most important contribution they make to their respective schools. They also consider it to be the hardest because it requires them to give more of themselves than any of their other roles and responsibilities. Many new heads are astonished at the extent to which they can affect the mood, the pace and the culture of their schools: the reality is that if a headteacher does not both extol and personify the aims, targets and standards that the organisation is aiming to meet and possibly exceed, the desire on the part of the staff and students to work hard and with purpose will almost certainly be diminished as a consequence.

This can put real pressures on school leaders. Headteachers, like everyone else, have private lives. They have families, they have rows and they sometimes have personal problems to overcome. However, if you are seen to be bringing these problems into the workplace, you may find some sympathy, some under-standing, initially but the tough lesson you have to learn is that that level of support will not last long, no matter how popular you are or successful you may be in the role. Sooner rather than later, a headteacher who keeps his or her head down will affect the feel-good culture of a school and standards will decline as a result. It is so important to keep all these things in mind when you are going about your day-to-day business. Get it wrong and it can badly affect staff/student morale. Get it right and it can make a massively positive impact on the working atmosphere.

Talking heads

Eleanor, a recently appointed head of a large primary school in the north east of England articulated a common problem that goes hand in hand with headship:

If I come into school with what my staff would describe as a 'long face' the word goes round the place like wildfire that I am not in a good mood and that people had better watch out. More often than not I am not smiling because I am just trying to sort something out in my mind or deciding when to do some shopping! I really believe that I am an approachable person who does not throw her weight around and tries desperately hard to be even tempered and fair minded at all times, even when provoked, but the status that goes with the job title seems to have a life of its own! I've also found that if I make a silly aside or attempt some humour at a colleague's expense, it can often backfire. Even the innocent question 'How are you?' can have teachers desperately looking for the hidden significance of such an apparently innocent enquiry!

Being around and being seen

The need for the physical presence of the head in the school in order for staff to feel valued and empowered was mentioned by several of our interviewees. One head I met echoed the need for headteachers to be in school, saying that she only felt the place 'settled' when she walked in the door. Although this can look as though headteachers are over-exaggerating the power and extent of their influence, the anecdotal evidence would suggest that they are not. It may be the case that the larger the school the less marked this is, because people do not necessarily come into contact with the head as much as they might in, for example, a small infant school.

Talking heads

Sue, the head of an inner-city primary school, said that she realised after two years that although her school had a terrific leadership team and was a happy and successful place, *it* needed *her* to be there. At first she thought that she was imagining this and over-emphasising the power of her own presence but she realised very quickly that she wasn't.

> This need to be there in person was made crystal clear to me when I took a semi-secondment at the National College of School Leadership, which meant that I was out of school two days a week. I was quite relaxed about doing this because I knew it was valuable professional development for me and that my leadership team were very experienced and quite capable of managing without me.
>
> After two terms my PA (someone whose views I both sought and trusted) came in to see me and asked if she could share something rather sensitive with me. I thought that she had some personal/family problem. Not at all! She simply said that the staff were missing me not being there. I was really surprised because I thought I was managing perfectly well on the three days I was at the school. However, the difference was that I was apparently no longer finding the time to get around the school, talk to people about all the day-to-day stuff (some of it pretty incidental and trivial!) that I did when I was there every day.
>
> What I realised was how important that aspect of my work was if I was to keep the staff and students feeling valued and positive about what they were doing. It was something I would never have picked up on if my PA had not had the honesty and courage to tell me how people were feeling. It was also a lesson that I never forgot.

Positive interactions: treating people as people

Good headteachers will always have at the forefront of their thinking that their role involves constant interactions with people – young, middle aged and even older! All these people will have needs of their own, some of which they will not acknowledge or perhaps even recognise as needs. The extent to which you manage these interactions, as head, will have a massive influence on the working atmosphere of the place.

At the heart of this is the need to treat all members of the organisation as individuals in their own right – no mean task if you happen to be in charge of a school that has 200+ staff and 1,500 or more students. Equally, it is no mean task either if you are running a small school with fewer than 150 students and staff in single figures because sensitivities can be prickly and feelings can run deep. Upset one influential member of staff in a small tightly knit infant school for example and the fall out can be immensely damaging.

Keeping people on side

As with so many aspects of headship there is no single formula for success. However, the following rules/guidelines may well be worth considering:

1 Wherever possible, get to know every member of staff by name and as many students as possible, even if your school is a very large comprehensive. People feel unloved and unwanted if the boss cannot even bother to remember their names.

2 Have a network of trusted colleagues who will keep you up to speed with what is going on. Your PA, if he or she is good, will normally be first rate at handing you useful information about staff personal upsets, failed marriages, out of school achievements, family illnesses, financial difficulties etc. Make sure that whenever appropriate you make gentle enquiries and offer support if it is needed.

3 Remember corridor conversations can be a rich source of information and allow you keep up to speed with what is happening in your school. If a member of staff tells you about a forthcoming operation or a graduation or a special event in their lives, follow that up with a further enquiry when the actual event has passed.

4 Wherever possible, acknowledge people's achievements or milestones in their particular careers or personal lives. It works wonders if you ask how an exam went or if someone's mother is out of hospital. It works equally well if you congratulate them for a particular assembly or on an effective display in their classroom. Show clearly that you are proud of what they have achieved.

5   Share a joke with people, particularly if it is at your own expense. Whenever possible, try to leave colleagues with a smile on their faces at the end of any conversation you have with them.

6   Do not be afraid to give people honest feedback, if that is what they want. It is always relatively easy to soften the blow when giving bad news but people will respect you more and trust you more if you tell them the truth.

7   Make sure that all your performance review procedures reflect the key aims and objectives of the school and tie in any performance rewards with tangible, challenging and measurable results. People only really appreciate pay rises they think they deserve!

8   Be sympathetic when it comes to compassionate leave if the request is understandable and reasonable. You will get so much more from your staff if you show that you have a human side and are prepared to bend the rules if it is the right thing to do. Classic examples would be requests to attend a child's first nativity play or a son or daughter's graduation. In most cases, asking the person concerned to sort out his or her own cover arrangements works well. This does not mean that you are regarded as a pushover and there may well be times when you refuse a request but never assume that a kindness shown by you will be seen as an act of weakness. It won't.

9   Wherever and whenever possible, thank people for what they have done – formally and informally. Of course, thanking people can be a pretty thankless task because you can guarantee that after a concert or a play you will thank 50 people but upset the three you failed to thank! However, if you are seen by staff as someone who goes out of your way to say thank you, it will be much appreciated and will spur those people on to do it again. Something as small as bringing cakes to the staffroom to celebrate successes can work wonders for staff morale!

This is by no means an exhaustive list but the above examples illustrate, it is hoped, the extent to which headteachers have to read situations carefully, use a great deal of emotional intelligence and try to make sure that their dealings with people will increase levels of motivation, make the school a nice place to work in and contribute to the feeling of purpose and energy that in this chapter we are describing as the 'buzz'.

Maintaining the 'feel-good' factor

This 'feel-good' factor that always inhabits successful schools is as vital and tangible as it is intangible and hard to quantify but it is without doubt the life-blood of any effective organisation and if it is lost, everyone suffers the fallout. There are, for example, any number of factors that can adversely affect the 'buzz' of a place:

- poor, confused communication
- mixed messages – especially from leadership
- public arguments
- disaffected factions who are anti-management on principle
- inadequate school building/insufficient kit
- negative, unfair media coverage
- no tea or coffee and poor food in the canteen
- unruly students who appear to be 'getting away with it'
- too many meetings.

The list goes on and on and we all, I am sure, recognise all or most of the above. Dealing constructively with each one and making sure that no irreparable damage is caused by them is a real challenge. It is not true to say that all of the above will be the responsibility of the headteacher to solve/resolve but allowing these negative factors to increase in strength and intensity is a threat that all headteachers need to see as a major part of their role. Staff and students will be expecting you to sort these things out and your street credibility will be badly damaged if you do not. As far as this list is concerned, possible solutions to some of those mentioned are detailed on the pages that follow.

Effective communication

Make sure that all communication is as clear and accessible as possible. It is always important to have the right amount of information circulating, in the right format, to the right people, at the right time. Too little too late is just as bad as too much too often! As for mixed messages from your leadership team, they can prove to be utterly corrosive. Although some staff might think that it is fun to see senior members of staff arguing with each other in public or openly criticising the head, the fact is that such behaviour can thoroughly de-motivate people and make them feel very unsettled. The most effective and respected leadership teams argue behind closed doors – often passionately – but present a united front at all other times.

Creating the right environment

The problem of an inadequate school building or insufficient resources can be very depressing but even in straightened times, good leaders will be able to do things that make people feel optimistic. An effective head will always be looking to access any and all funding streams even though the strike rate is frustratingly poor much of the time. Knowing that you as a head are not just shrugging your shoulders and making empty noises expressing sympathy, can give out a very upbeat message to staff and students. And when one of these funding bids is successful or when a significant sponsor is found, the positive spin-offs are immense! Creating and maintaining a professional working atmosphere by making sure that, whenever possible, classrooms are painted, display boards are kept attractive and up to date, the day-to-day cleaning is as good as it can be and broken doors, windows and furniture are replaced quickly, makes all the difference.

Making meetings work

We all know that 'meetingitis' is a common illness in many organisations. Honda, the Japanese car company, introduced a policy several years ago that there were to be no chairs at any meetings and that all those attending that meeting would have to stand for the duration. Almost overnight, meetings became more focused and much shorter. David Middlewood, Jackie Beere and I (2005, p.8) explored this idea in detail in describing their idea of a learning school: 'A large number of people think most effectively when they walk around...so it makes no sense to insist that everyone sits at a table and therefore impose one learning style on everyone.'

Even doing away with the seemingly obligatory refreshments can make a significant difference to the timing and mood of meetings. People can always bring their own tea or coffee to a meeting if that is their wish. Similarly, making sure that meetings are well publicised, well documented, chaired and minuted and secure positive outcomes will make all the difference.

Staff welfare

Some organisations succeed in getting many of the big decisions right but manage to upset their staff by missing out on some of the finer details. It is, for example, very easy to provide staff with decent lunchtime menus with plenty of choice (it is astonishing how many schools still allow caterers to fall short of acceptable standards) and free tea and coffee. However, some schools still charge for refreshments or only provide horrible little machines that make nothing drinkable.

I know of one staff office where everyone (including the head) contributed to a tea/coffee/biscuit fund each month. As if this was not demeaning enough, the head went on a two-week trip to Canada and then insisted on his return that they return half his monthly allowance! Although examples like this may appear trite, the negative fallout among staff can be immense. At the other end of the scale, there are schools that provide free postgraduate studies for all staff, offer one-off financial incentives for outstanding service and free private healthcare. Although the latter example may appear to be over-generous, it is anything but – simply because the heads who have introduced very cost-effective private healthcare schemes report much better attendance among staff and much more rapid solutions to medical problems.

Dealing with the disaffected

Of course, there is in virtually every school a small group of people who will never be satisfied and who will forever be looking for the negative in all and every situation. They certainly do not want to have anything to do with 'buzz'! Rather, they are people who view 'management' with mistrust and distaste and who will interpret all your efforts to convince them otherwise as devious underhand tactics to win them over in order to do them down.

They can, if poorly managed, wield a power and influence entirely dispro-portionate to their worth. They will often hijack meetings, spread rumour and mischief in the staffroom and try very hard to bring any new staff into their way of thinking. Many heads have said how they have witnessed cynical, longer-serving members of staff 'turning' extremely promising young members of staff into cynics themselves. Even worse, people like this can force talented young entrants out of the school and even out of the profession.

The secret is not to let the minority grow and to make sure that there are positive voices in the staffroom that are prepared to challenge their negativity. The other trick is to give them very little real meat to complain about. You do this by making sure that the ideas you put forward, the innovations you introduce and the changes you make (see Chapter 8) gain widespread approval. By so doing, you make their complaints, objections and criticisms appear so much more ridiculous.

If you can win one or more of them over by recognising a quality or talent they may have and promoting it publicly, you can make a real hit. Sometimes you are presented with the chance of winning over one of the talented sceptics by giving them extra paid responsibilities and bringing them on side as a consequence. This is gold dust in terms of your own approval rating and the positive effect it will have on the working atmosphere of the school.

Pause for thought

- Remember that the role and status of headship can have a life of its own and can exert an influence way beyond any other position in school. Be aware of how much you can affect a member of staff or student negatively and/or positively by what you say and how you behave.
- There are many factors – even in very happy successful schools – that can impact negatively on the 'buzz' of a school. How you deal with these can make all the difference to the 'feel' of the school and your own credit rating among the staff and students.
- There is no such thing as an innocent aside in headship! Your impact on the morale of the staff in particular is entirely disproportionate to the actual job you are doing.

Maintaining the momentum

When you are in the school, never underestimate the degree of influence – positive or negative – you can have on it. Lee Iacocca, the General Manager of Chrysler, once commented that he had always found the speed of the boss to be the speed of the team. In this one observation he has captured both the significance and challenge of this particular strand of leadership. We all know that coasting schools are failing schools and that if any organisation is content with its current performance it will see that performance deteriorate fairly rapidly.

To keep a school buzzing, it is essential for all staff and students to maintain a sense that things are happening and changing (for the better) and that no one is promoting complacency. Even though students might claim that they would like a quiet life at school and that they resent new initiatives and too much change, they resent much more the feeling that their school is not going anywhere and that everything is predictable, pedestrian and uninspiring. In my experience, the vast majority of students want to feel proud of their school and its published successes.

Talking heads

Christopher, the head of an outstandingly successful mixed comprehensive in Gloucestershire, feels very strongly that students need to feel energised by their school:

> I am really keen that we shouldn't just 'buzz' about results; we should 'buzz' about everything that's happening. You can get the kids involved in lots of national competitions which are centred on learning for its own sake. I try to make sure that I attend all the concerts and give all the prizes out because I believe that my presence confirms the point of the exercise and the value of the achievement in the students' (and the staff's) eyes.

> We have a termly magazine that promotes and celebrates the students' achievements and I'm always looking for ways to congratulate the students formally and informally and make them feel good about what they have done and even more important, about themselves. None of this is especially revolutionary of course but I think where we score heavily is the degree to which we do this and the consistency with which we praise staff and students. In my experience there are very few people who will not welcome praise and be buoyed up by it. I absolutely believe and, I hope, promote the mantra that an ounce of praise is worth a ton of criticism.

Time and time again in our interviews with headteachers, this sense of needing to keep things moving along was frequently noted as an essential skill for senior leaders. This does not mean that no one in the organisation will get on and do things if the head is not there prodding them. Indeed, I have come across examples (not many in truth!) where staff are compelled to do things in spite of rather than because of the leadership culture. But this is rare. Everyone working in a school needs to feel that the momentum and the drive is being led by the headteacher. If the head is not buzzing with enthusiasm, the school will not be an exciting place to be. Too much excitement and enthusiasm can, of course, also be counter-productive and headteachers who are always promising to deliver wonderful things but never in reality do so can be disastrously irritating and de-motivating.

Some of the comments made by interviewees regarding this area of their work are worth sharing. For example:

- 'I always want the school to have a challenge. I want the ethos to be supportive but if it's too cosy we lose the spirit of adventure that I consider to be an essential element in school improvement.'

- 'Whoever leads, at whatever level, must believe passionately in the possibility of doing great things and making the place better. Genetic imprinting of this concept is not essential. Late converts should be readily accepted.'

- 'Keeping the momentum going is my primary role. I think headteachers are pivotal in this regard. The drive and direction comes from them. The leadership team need to enrich that drive and direction.'

- It's a can-do culture at my school but it's that culture because we never give the impression that we're having time out in order to recover! I always look as if I'm feeling upbeat and positive about any and everything even if inside I'm feeling anything but…!'

- 'Feeling upbeat and enthusiastic about what is going on is, of course, to some extent an act. But it's a very important act.'

- 'You need to be consistently and rigorously enthusiastic. You have to be out and about, constantly challenging and taking a genuine interest in what is going on. Having been a head for some years now I really recognise how absolutely essential that is.'

- 'Remember, a school, like a dog, takes on the personality of its boss. If you are not eagerly looking for the next challenge, no one else will be.'

- 'I have to be the eternal optimist. Strangely, I've noticed that the fact I am always the optimist allows the rest of the staff the luxury of being slightly pessimistic on occasions, secure in the knowledge that they can come to me and get the positive spin on a situation. That can be really tough!'

Creating a sense of excitement and anticipation

It is easy to slip into a culture where everything is 'OK' and that there is no real need to do anything much to keep things ticking over. However, we all know that something left to tick over can in fact be a time bomb and that schools that fall into this trap are almost invariably on a path to self destruction. The way to avoid this of course is to create and sustain the 'buzz'. Although it may seem slightly heretical to say it, school improvement can sometimes require a little gentle trickery. Astute headteachers will introduce schemes and promote ideas that will keep people on their toes and will create a sense of excitement and anticipation even when the cold facts do not quite justify the optimism. There is absolutely nothing wrong with doing this on occasions but it becomes less effective the longer it goes on.

The 'big idea'

The concept of the 'big idea' was first introduced to me by a highly effective headteacher of a mixed comprehensive in the south east of England. He stressed time and time again that at the start of each new academic it was vital that staff did not get into the mindset that they were on the treadmill once again, that they had a series of familiar landmarks to negotiate and hurdles to overcome and that by the end of the year nothing much will have changed. That mood is as easy to cultivate as it is difficult to break. One way of ensuring that each year is seen as a new challenge is to introduce something which is innovative, which is school-wide and which captures the imagination of most if not all the staff.

The innovation does not have to be especially revolutionary. It could for example, centre on a determination for the coming year to ensure that all subject areas do something new and vital in their classroom spaces to reflect, embrace and celebrate their respective curriculum areas. I remember one particular head who took it even further with his leadership team and divided the year into three sessions, each of which, without fail, was vitally important in maintaining the school's momentum. His deputy head in his leaving speech, after what were by all accounts four heady and exciting years, said that he had just completed his thirteenth crucial term! However, looking back, he realised how important this particular apprenticeship was in helping him secure his first headship.

Generating this sense that the school is entering a new exciting phase in its development can be infectious. Well-received innovations from leadership teams, particularly if they are well managed and are seen to be instrumental in improving and refining the quality of service the school is providing, will help create a culture where other members of staff will be inspired to try something new. A dynamic headteacher will grasp this opportunity with both hands because if you have a culture of 'positive restlessness', as one head described to us, you will have a sizeable minority of staff – perhaps more – who will be coming up to you with a smile on their faces saying 'I've got an idea!' As one of our interviewees put it:

'Welcome entrepreneurs. Make your school distinctive by encouraging eccentrics who want to open on Saturdays and move Year 7 to France for a month'.

Once you have established a mood in the school where significant numbers of people are thinking about how to keep things upbeat, where magnificent failure is applauded and whacky ideas are greeted with enthusiasm, you will have succeeded in cementing the buzz culture into the school. Equally important is to maintain a learning philosophy where *all* staff – not just teachers – are involved in making the learning effective. The very environment of the school matters, so it follows that the cleaner, the caretaker, the catering staff, the office administrators and the technicians all have a role to play. You know you are in an effective school when you talk to people who are not in the classroom every day and yet they are quite clear about the school's central philosophies and aims. Those schools that have systems in place to encourage non-teaching staff and fellow students for example to mentor students, take classes, do research into learning styles and be involved in residentials will be demonstrating every day that learning is a life-long occupation and everyone is capable of making a contribution. 'Everyone a teacher, everyone a learner' is a powerful mantra to promote!

By so doing, although you as head will still have a crucial role in maintaining the school's momentum, you will not have the sole responsibility for sustaining or for generating the ideas. This is most probably what Sergiovanni (1991) was implying when he said that vision should not be constructed as a strategic plan that functions as a road map charting the turns needed to reach a specific reality. It should be viewed more as a compass that points the direction to be taken, that inspires enthusiasm and allows people to buy into and take part in the shaping of the way. How true! Few things are as gratifying for a head than to walk round the school and see staff and students trying out new ideas and running with off-the-wall initiatives that they intuitively believe reflect the values and the culture of the school. Some heads worry if they are not aware of everything that is going on in their schools. The best heads worry if they do.

Pause for thought

- Consider the extent to which you have to lead by example. You need to be the 'buzz leader' even when you feel anything but! Remember too that how you are and how you look will be constantly monitored by everyone you deal with.
- Never lose sight of the fact the people you are leading are individuals in their own right, all with their own needs, agendas and aspirations. Wherever possible, make them feel that you recognise and acknowledge that.
- Do not assume that you have to come up with all the ideas. Effective heads provide the stimulus and the context to encourage all members of staff to suggest innovations and ideas that will move things on.

Whole-school buzz

So far this chapter has dealt primarily with strategies to ensure that there is a 'buzz' in the staffroom and that all staff feel challenged and valued. There is of course the equal challenge of making sure that the students feel the same way. After all, when all is said and done, it is patently of no use to have incredibly enthusiastic staff skipping out of the staffrooms to take their next lesson, only to be greeted by a group of apathetic, negative, switched off young people who believe that the school is a dump!

Much of what applies to staff applies equally to students. Making them feel valued, giving them opportunities to pursure their own agendas and listening to their needs, concerns and ideas will of course make all the difference. Effective headteachers will always have at the forefront of their thinking the need to be providing students at all times with a stimulating environment that will make them keen to learn.

The curriculum

In the context of this chapter, the need to have a curriculum that is tailored to meet the strengths and aspirations of the students is a given. No school is going to have a buzz about it if the teaching is pedestrian and the students are beaten (metaphorically!) into submission every day. However, even when the teaching and learning are consistently good, there are ways in which the learning environment can be given that extra edge and bite. The best schools are always risk takers by nature and there is no harm whatsoever in challenging the traditional conventions of how lessons can or should be delivered.

One school in South Yorkshire has, for example, completely moved away from the traditional weekly timetabled curriculum. In its place, the school has a group of learning zones, the students have a work desk, a series of tasks that they need to complete each week and plenty of advice from teachers about what they need to have achieved by the end of the week. How they do that, however, is largely up to them. The headteacher discovered that when you give students that degree of freedom, for example, they select when they have to attend a maths tutorial in order to complete an assignment and they devise and prioritise their work schedule, the learning culture changes dramatically. Because the students own their own learning, they learn more. Other examples of more imaginative use of learning time include:

- vertical house/teaching groups
- days divided into two three-hour teaching sessions
- enrichment sessions before and after the school day
- students teaching teachers
- whole-school days targeted at creativity workshops
- holiday or weekend teaching and revision lessons
- extended residentials
- learning conferences (e.g. TED) and training days run by students
- international curriculum exchanges.

In *Creating a Learning School* (2005) we offered many more illustrations of this innovative approach to learning. The message in all this is that by constantly looking at ways in which to make the learning more real and by involving the students in their own learning, any school is much more likely to keep the mood upbeat and vibrant.

Student voice

Schools are increasingly looking to their learners to participate in and comment on the range and quality of what is being offered. Clearly this makes sense on a number of levels. Students are, for example, very good at identifying what does and what does not work in terms of teaching and learning. They can also invariably spot a poor teacher at ten miles! For this reason an increasing number of schools are now encouraging students to help in appointing staff, take part in training sessions, evaluate the quality of teaching and learning by doing lesson observations and becoming much more actively involved in operational and governance matters.

The energy coming from this is the degree to which students will own initiatives and major decisions and become partners in the day-to-day delivery of the whole curriculum. As far as they are concerned, it no longer becomes 'your teaching' and 'my learning' but rather 'our learning'. The doctor/patient model is replaced by a learning partnership culture centred on mutual respect.

It is not right to assume that young people have to be a certain age before they can make a valid and valuable contribution to the effectiveness of a school. Many primary heads have talked enthusiastically and proudly about how their pupils take on responsibilities in and around the school and about how perceptive and relevant their views are when it comes to what makes for good teaching and learning. Quite simply, if young people of all ages feel that their views and interests are being taken into account and that the consultation is genuine, they will be much more knowledgeable and fired up about the direction the school is taking. There's the buzz!

The reward/celebration culture

It is therefore very important, as Chris suggested (page 128), to make staff feel valued; celebrating their achievements and thanking them for their efforts makes all the difference. The same applies to students of course. Schools should take every opportunity to recognise and reward student achievement. It is not possible to go into great detail here about how this can be done but, for example, a formal and informal culture of assemblies, special events and awards can make all the difference. Making students feel good about their school can make them feel good about themselves.

If the students have achieved really good exam results, shout it from the rooftops! Don't be confined to the somewhat repetitive and well-worn phrases in the local newspaper. Make sure the message is heard around the school. Hand out cakes and chocolate if you like! Put a huge banner at the front of the school saying 'Congratulations' in large letters. One school reception area I visited displays their unquestionably excellent results for all to see. After each headline there is the question 'Why on earth would you want to study anywhere else?!' That's clever.

Talking heads

Iain, a recently retired headteacher of what had been a seriously underper-forming large mixed comprehensive in Manchester, illustrated this technique very effectively:

> I used to mentor students in their GCSE year who were predicted to undera-chieve by as much as two grades. I met with them every week and they became my 'two grade heroes' insofar as they were looking to improve on predictions by at least two grades. If I ever saw them in the corridors or having lunch with their friends I would always call out 'How are my two grade heroes?!'

> The reaction was invariably the same: initial embarrassment at being singled out publicly in this way by the head followed by a slight smile as they acknowledged that they were the specific targets of my attention. By constantly referring to them in this way, I managed to sow in their minds the fact that they were two grade heroes and that is what they would be in their forthcoming examinations. I'm pleased to say that the success rate was impressive. Giving them the recognition and belief gave them the motivation and the confidence to prove me right.

Providing an environment that will create the buzz

Creating the right climate for people to feel upbeat has not a little to do with subliminal advertising. If you display around your school the visual evidence of its achievements and its standing in the local/regional community, the very nature and simplicity of the message is internalised by all who work there. People talk a lot about the power of mission statements in this regard but if truth be told, most of them are of little or no value. Collins and Porras (1991) consider most mission statements to be terribly ineffective as a compelling guiding force because they do not grab people in the gut and motivate them to work toward a common end.

I was reminded of how true it is that most mission statements are no more than a boring stream of words when I was doing a one-day training session at a boys' comprehensive in Northamptonshire with a large group of staff and students. As part of the day's training, I asked what the school's mission statement was, fully expecting everyone to shrug their shoulders and say nothing or come spout forth a boring stream of words. Instead, all the staff and all the students shouted out as one 'Passion for learning!' That unity of thinking gave out a powerful message and showed very effectively how this school was the exception to the rule!

Early on in my second headship we had an Ofsted inspection. The school received a very positive report and the staff were much encouraged when the inspectors described the school as a place where it was 'cool to learn'. The strap-line 'cool to learn' immediately went all over the school – on doors, on windows, on walls – in fact, the students frequently said that they were tired of seeing it! However tired they were, they were still internalising the message.

One of this country's top private schools has a similar strap-line. The motto there is 'It's cool to be clever'. The head told us that whereas 20 years ago any student who chose to waste his time, the significant fees and the incredible opportunities on offer by managing to fail everything was seen by other students as being pretty cool. Now, he says, the students would consider him to be pretty stupid. That represents a telling and profound change in culture.

There are any number of ways of creating this buzzing atmosphere. Nowadays there are companies who will (at no great cost) put huge impressive illustrations, pictures and slogans all over your school that trumpet aspiration and achievement. An academy David visited had the name of the school etched out across one huge wall in the foyer that was made up of the faces of every single child in the school. The line underneath was 'We love our school'. Powerful stuff. In the design department there were large pictures of great designers, from Leonardo da Vinci to Dyson and alongside their pictures were inspirational quotes about the beauty of design.

In another school one whole wall was taken up by a picture that showed a huge barren mountain, at the very top of which was a tree. Underneath, in large letters was 'Yes you can!' Cynics will quickly dismiss such images as rather tasteless and ineffective but I disagree. Filling your school with positive images and thoughts can have an immensely powerful effect on the feel-good, upbeat culture of the place and make people proud to work there. That can make such a difference.

Conclusion

All schools will of course have their own working practices and cultures, and what works for one school might not work for another. This is where the head's judgement is crucial. Headteachers need to know and understand what will and will not work in their respective schools. However, the clear message of this chapter is that keeping a 'buzz' in your school is not something that can be left to chance. The topic needs constant re-visiting and re-working and everything possible needs to be done to ensure that everyone working in the organisation comes into work each day with a sense of purpose and anticipation. Although the challenge of achieving that can be daunting on occasions, the rewards can be measurable and immeasurable.

Action points

- Make sure, particularly if you are new in post, that you get out to other schools that have a reputation for having a 'buzz' and look to steal any and all of their ideas.

- Employ a decent architect who understands schools and who will, if the funding permits, be able to create inspiring learning spaces for your staff and students.

- Look for the pioneers in the staffroom and encourage them to take risks. Celebrate their successes and sympathise with their failures.

- Never miss an opportunity to advance the agenda or heighten expectations. Never let the grass grow under your feet and always be annoyed if another school comes up with a great idea that you should have thought of first!

- Always make sure that you do whatever you can to support an idea that has effective learning at its heart. Wherever possible, do not allow funding to be the deciding issue.

- Get to know who the movers and shakers are in your area – the people who make things happen. Invite them into school and exploit them as much as you can. They will be amenable if they see can see something in it for themselves.

- Never stop celebrating achievements or dishing out thanks. Do everything you can to make everyone in your school proud to be working there.

8 How to manage change

This chapter considers the challenges, apprehensions and strategies that come into play when as a leader you are contemplating, planning, introducing and effecting change. It addresses:

- The underlying principles and practices governing successful change.
- Some of the most common pitfalls.
- Examples from practice of where change worked well and why.
- Examples from practice where change went badly wrong and why.
- How to rescue unsuccessful change and turn a threat into an opportunity.

The place and importance of change

As a topic, 'managing change' is almost as popular as leadership on many library shelves and consequently large number of articles, books and training manuals have been written about how to change things effectively, i.e. how to make things better. In our view, the major reason for this is because successful leaders will, by definition, effect successful change and by so doing exercise one of their most important functions.

In spite of this, you hear many stories in staffrooms and at meetings/conferences, and indeed they are borne out by research, of where this vitally important part of a leader's work appears to be far less successful than it could or should have been and the consequences are far-reaching and potentially extremely damaging. Few things, for example, are more debilitating and de-motivating than being involved in a lengthy and strenuous process of change that results in a general feeling throughout the organisation that things were much better before all the change started. The resulting damage to a leader's street credibility can be terminal.

It's not that difficult!

There are many models of managing change in the literature of both the academic and business world and the best of them are logical, sensible and steeped in common sense. What they tend to say is that managing change is nowhere near as complex and difficult as some might have us believe. Some key points to bear in mind in order to avoid some of the common pitfalls include:

- Too few headteachers listen to the 'if it ain't broke, don't fix it' mantra when taking on a first or new headship.

- There seems to be an in-built assumption on the part of some incoming heads that they will have to change just about everything in the first six months of their tenure if they are going to be judged as a dynamic, successful appointment or – even worse – 'doing what they have been paid to do'.

- Some leaders come into schools with a pre-determined template of what they consider to be a successful school. They move rapidly to adapt everything about the school they are now running to match their own inevitably biased views of what works and what does not.

- Change should never be a surprise for those who the change affects – welcome or unwelcome.

- Significant, transformational change will not work effectively if it is not owned and understood by those who are expected to implement and manage that change.

By failing to recognise any of the above, school leaders run the risk of changing things that are already working very well and are perceived by staff and students to be strengths and introduce practices and innovations that appear to reduce the school's effectiveness. The secret is only to introduce change if you are confident that:

- it is needed
- it will work.

As Heath and Heath (2010) put it: 'Change is easier if you know where you're going and why it's worth it'. Failure to observe, what is on the face of it, a very simple observation can seriously tarnish a headteacher's reputation for managing change effectively.

Talking heads

Sarah, a head of a large comprehensive in the north of England, recalled one of the changes she made more by accident than design:

One of the decisions I made very quickly when I began my second headship was to remove bells. The college had 360 bells each week and I had not worked in a school that had bells for over 20 years – and I could not be doing with them. However, bearing in mind the importance of context, I needed to know in my own mind that removing the bells would improve the feel and atmosphere of the place. As a 14–19 school there was no excuse for anyone to say that they needed a bell to remind them to move and we introduced the concept of no bells by arguing that the students would not have bells in the workplace or at university so getting used to managing your own time well was good preparation for the next stage in their lives.

I put up the suggestion prior to taking up the post and unsurprisingly there was some significant opposition (more in fact than I had anticipated) from the staff who did not relish the idea of having the bells taken out. Indeed, such was the level and intensity of the opposition that I decided to wait for a few weeks before making the change. On my first day at the school everything seemed to be a slight blur from the outset – a common experience for heads new in post – and it was not until near the end of the first morning that I realised that there had been no bells sounded.

When I called one of the premises officers in to ask what had happened he looked somewhat blankly at me and said that he had been told that I did not like bells so he had switched them off! The morning had gone like clockwork (no pun intended!) and bells were never reintroduced. I know that if it was suggested that they return there would be a revolution – from the students as well as the staff.

Understanding the context when making change

What works for one school will not necessarily work for another. My second headship led me to a school that was considered to be the county's flagship comprehensive. Regularly topping the examination league tables, it enjoyed a national reputation for innovation and cutting-edge practice. The school was huge with well over 2,000 students, the majority of whom came from middle/ upper middle class backgrounds and who were in the main confident, articulate and keen to succeed. In this regard it was very different from my first headship which was in a smaller school, located in the middle of a more deprived working class environment where expectations were generally lower and where the aspirations of the parents were much less broad and informed.

I mention this to illustrate the importance of context when you are considering whether or not to make a change to the status quo. When it became clear in my first school, a medium sized mixed comprehensive in a very challenging part of Northamptonshire, that student behaviour was an issue, the staff went to great lengths to introduce Lee Canter's (1992) assertive discipline (sometimes referred to as D4L: Discipline for Learning) into the school. They had judged, rightly as it turned out, that the students would respond well to the transparency and rigidity of the scheme that centred on consistency set alongside clear rewards and consequences.

It worked for the students because as a general rule they needed and secretly welcomed the fact that if they stepped out of line certain things would happen and if they did well, their efforts would be publicly acknowledged. It worked for the staff, many of whom were relatively new to the profession, because it gave them a clear set of rules and expectations to use. In some ways, it relieved the pressure on them to decide how to respond to the range of situations they might well face in what could be a quite tough learning environment. It was without doubt one of the most successful changes the school introduced – a development which, with one or two additions and amendments, is still apparently working well, nearly ten years later.

If I had introduced the same programme into my second school, however, it would almost certainly have been a disaster because the context was fundamentally different. Many more of the staff were experienced professionals who had worked at the school for some time. The students were in the main, mature and motivated and enjoyed coming to school (called, perhaps significantly, a 'college') and would have reacted very negatively to being subjected to a scheme which they would have perceived to be unnecessarily rigid.

In this college, the success it enjoyed was based as much as anything on a culture of learning, where the quality of the relationships that existed between teacher and learner were central to everything that went on. The fact that people were not restricted and/or shoe-horned into a disciplinary scheme that allowed for little or no personal interpretation of how to deal with behaviour was, in this school's cultural context, key to establishing and maintaining a positive working atmosphere in the classroom. A formula-driven disciplinary system would have damaged and undermined the tangible sense of trust and mutual respect that had become one of the school's abiding strengths.

If it ain't broke…

Some practices already existing in a school will seem strange and probably unnecessary to the incoming leader, but that leader needs to realise they came into being for a reason and have survived for a reason. So sweep them away at your peril! These are known as the 'rituals' in the literature on organisational culture. Any examination of our own daily lives soon shows that we all practise certain rituals, because – well, because we do!

There is therefore much to be said for recognising and applauding that which is working really well and which has the confidence and support of staff and students and not removing it because it was not your idea! After all, any sensible head will firstly acknowledge that successful schools do not become or remain successful by chance. Good schools will have established practices that work and therefore any changes or modifications to such practices will need to be made sensitively in a context of recognising and understanding the pulse of the organisation and knowing what innovations are going to complement and develop rather than confront existing practice. Equally, good schools can have practices which are judged to be perfectly sound but are not necessarily in the best interests of the people working in them. There is absolutely no reason why these should not be confronted.

The implicit dangers in maintaining the status quo

This does not mean that headteachers should spend most of their time concentrating on practising what is termed 'transactional management'. They have not been appointed to such an important position to just keep things ticking over. When you take on a successful school you know that the continued success of that school will very largely depend on the nature and the quality of the changes that are made. The mantra 'For everything to remain the same, everything must change' is a valuable and necessary philosophy for all school leaders to keep at the centre of their thinking.

Talking heads

Stewart, the head of a medium sized comprehensive school in the Midlands, talked about how he reacted to a unique feature of the school he took on:

My predecessor, an unapologetic traditionalist, had been at the school for over 20 years and had a profound influence on the culture of the place – not all of it positive in my view. As a practising Quaker, he passionately believed in the place and strength of personal, quiet reflection and for this reason had put in place year assemblies where the students entered the hall in silence, sat in silence for ten minutes and then left in silence. To say that I was cynical about this would have been an understatement!

As the head was telling me about these 'Reflections' as the assemblies were known, I pictured in my mind the sniggering, secret texting, face pulling and misbehaving that I was sure would be going on in these sessions. Imagine my surprise therefore when I attended the first of these assemblies and experienced a real sense of peace and reflection. The fact was that they had become such an integral part of the culture that they were valued and respected by everyone taking part in them. I realised that it would be madness to change them and I did not. I have never regretted that decision and 'Reflections' have continued to be an important and highly valued feature of what makes the school what it is.

Certain parts of a headteacher's weekly routine will of course involve transactional matters: the bureaucracy, the daily briefings, managing exams, the form filling, the letters, the inevitable financial returns and the like are inescapable realities of headship (an area explored in more detail in Chapters 5 and 6), but it is deceptively easy, the longer you are in the role, to make these aspects of the job your main focus and that is a real danger.

I'm not going to change anything!

Ian, one of our interviewees, remembers a new head coming to a school where he was working as a head of year. In his first staff meeting (a pivotal, daunting moment in any head's tenure!) he announced grandly and unequivocally that he would not change anything for a year. As a young teacher at the time that sounded rather reassuring. The school was a pleasant comfortable place to be and the fact that this was the late 1970s meant that external accountability was a distant glimmer on the horizon.

Needless to say, the staff were feeling very apprehensive about this new head in the wake of a long-serving head who had kept things fairly consistent and constant for the whole of his time there. Here was a man they thought, who was going to maintain the status quo, not shake things up too much and pretty much leave us alone to get on with things – at least until he had developed a clear view of the school's strengths and weaknesses.

Now of course with the benefit of hindsight, such a clear statement of intent on his part should have sounded real warning bells. Headteachers who publicly proclaim that they will not change anything for a year (why a year specifically?) are actually saying that they will not change anything much at all – ever – which is what in fact happened in this instance. What Ian (who fortunately left the school) had seen as a happy, untroubled school that did not spend any real time evaluating and challenging the quality of what it was doing was, in fact, not a good school at all. It was a coasting and unspectacular place that was failing its students in a fairly spectacular way. The school plodded on for a few years under this head's transactional, uninspiring and cautious leadership before sinking in to a general decline that finally found it failing its inspection and being taken in to special measures.

Pause for thought

- Remember that any perceived or managed change needs to be (and be seen to be) a change for the better; even more important, people other than you need to see it as an improvement on what was there before.
- For a new headteacher, there is an expectation from others that change will happen but there are real dangers in introducing significant change too quickly. Any early changes must either be rooted in your own

deep-seated beliefs or be clear and persuasive responses to glaringly obvious shortcomings.

- Always remember how important context is. A successful and well-received innovation in one school can have quite the opposite impact in another one: any anticipated change must be closely linked to the known recipients of that change.
- What worked so well in your previous school or college will not necessarily translate easily to your new one, and may be resented by some simply because it is from that school.

Knowing when to make changes

I have already talked about the dangers of acting too quickly. Equally there are dangers in not acting quickly enough. The head who decided not to change anything for a year (mentioned above) was falling into the trap of not making the distinction between what is just simply not good practice and what practice could and should be improved over a sustained period. For example, when David took on his headship, corporal punishment was still practised in schools and in this particular school, it was valued by many staff and many of the parents to be exactly what young people needed to teach them possibly the most important lesson (in their view) that they were going to learn at the school: behave or else!

Corporal punishment was anathema to David and he made the decision from the outset that it was no longer going to be used as a tool for maintaining order – not of course that it ever did. David came in for a lot of criticism from many quarters inside and outside of the school for advocating what they considered to be such a dangerous departure from what the school did 'well' and believed in. The idea that young people might behave better if they were engaged in learning instead was outside some people's fields of reference.

In the event, he overcame the criticism and eventually won over the staff, students and the local community (vindicated by the fact that the system was outlawed legally within two years). The significant point of all this is that there is no way that David would have waited for a year before taking this action. He had been encouraged in his determination to make that change through the words of an experienced educationalist who made the point that there are always in our own moral codes things 'up with which I cannot put!'.

This has got to change!

When you talk to senior leaders about their views on education they will soon mention philosophies and practices in education that they either passionately advocate or equally passionately reject. All these people will have taken on schools that in all probability did things that fell into both categories. The ones that were unacceptable would, if the head is a strong leader, have been the first to be changed or eliminated – most probably with little or no consultation.

I cannot tolerate this at any cost...

If you met with a group of heads and asked them what unacceptable practices or traditions they had to confront very early on in their headship there would almost certainly be a good measure of agreement. Simple examples would probably include:

- inappropriate dress
- anti-social corridor behaviour (staff as well as students!)
- poor attendance and punctuality (staff as well as students!)
- litter/smoking/bad language/graffiti
- ineffectual or non-existent marking of work
- inconsistent practice
- poor community relationships.

The list could of course be much longer but the point is that there are occasions when change needs to be made unilaterally, without consultation but with clear explanation. Some heads make the mistake of assuming that to introduce anything new requires automatic consultation 'with all relevant stakeholders' if the innovation is to be successful. But this is not true. People expect leaders to do their job and there will be times when that means telling people what you are going to do.

Research has shown (see Chapter 1) that teachers are difficult to please because they want consultation *and* to be given clear direction! In fact, staff and students rarely if ever resent clear decision-making that makes sense and that works and they respect leaders who have the courage of their convictions. The key, as always, is to make sure that when such actions are taken, the results of those actions are seen to be an improvement on what had been in place before. Of course the extent to which that will happen does depend a great deal on the cultural context within which the school operates – an area that requires greater examination.

Talking heads

Brian, a retired head, told me of an incident early in his own headship which illustrates well the necessity of making some changes very early on in post:

> I had worked for some years in London in a forward-looking city comprehensive that prided itself on being as status free as possible. The headteacher despised anything that smacked of unnecessary hierarchy and particularly disliked the practice of queue-jumping or leaving students outside staffrooms waiting for a reply to a question because the member of staff concerned was having his or her coffee.
>
> It did not take me long to realise that no such philosophy existed at the school. At break-time there were groups of students stood patiently outside the staffroom (clearly used to it!) waiting for staff to come out to talk to them and in the canteen at lunchtime I witnessed children being kept for nearly 15 minutes in a dinner queue while as many as 20 members of staff pushed in front of them to get served.
>
> The look of subdued resignation on the faces of the students on both occasions said a lot to me about what was wrong with the school's culture. I decided there and then to hold an emergency staff meeting at the end of the day to tell staff that, with immediate effect, everyone would queue properly and there would be no pushing in. Students would furthermore not be left outside the staffroom for the whole of break-time waiting to be seen by a member of staff. I also made it clear to the leadership team that I needed and expected their support in implementing these changes.
>
> Fortunately the leadership team were very supportive, not least because they could see how passionately I felt about this. Even though the reaction from the staff was initially hostile, after a while it became the norm and the looks of appreciation on the students' faces convinced me – not that I needed convincing – that I had done the right thing by making the change quickly and brooking no argument.

Creating the culture for positive change

An interesting question to pose when discussing the management of change is why some schools see change as an opportunity and others see it as a threat. This is particularly relevant in view of the fact that over the years, quite rightly on some occasions, teachers have bemoaned the nature, frequency and ill-prepared nature of changes to practice that have been put forward by various government departments. Even though all the evidence to date supports the view that teachers are more naturally resistant to change imposed from 'on high', they are in fact very good at dealing with those changes even though they manage to do so in spite of rather than because of the support they receive from local, regional or national government.

However, if you talk to headteachers about how they have managed change, some will praise their staff for being adventurous and entrepreneurial while others will complain bitterly about the fact that their staff are stuck in their ways and resistant to any attempts to change things for the better. The reason why some schools are much better than others at introducing change is, I believe, very largely dependent on the culture that has been established. That culture does not just happen by chance. When you consider why some schools positively relish change and some positively resist it, key features of both types of schools emerge.

When change is a threat

Schools that are instinctively resistant to change tend to have:

- a leadership culture or style that is predominantly autocratic in tone and approach
- high accountability alongside high blame
- a 'directing' rather than 'coaching' approach to staff development
- staff who generally prefer top-down change in which they have little or no part or interest
- a tendency to blame the students for any real or perceived shortcomings
- a good deal of interpersonal tension among significant numbers of staff
- a pervading sense that 'OK' is 'OK'
- plenty of personal agendas and lots of micro-politics (including destructive corridor conversations!)
- teacher-centred rather than student-centred priorities.

When change is an opportunity

Those schools that relish change reflect the following:

- a clear vision and clarity of purpose
- high expectations alongside low blame
- understood and owned organisational aims and objectives
- an in-built confidence in the quality of guidance and support for staff and students
- a leadership culture that is distributive and coaching in tone and approach
- staff and students feeling valued and whose opinions are regularly sought and often acted upon
- student-centred priorities
- continued re-visiting and re-focusing on the key underpinning principles and practices permeating the organisation.

These lists could be longer of course, but the key difference between schools that relish change and those that fear it is most aptly summed up by Michael Fullan's (1992) observation that change is more effective when it is done *by* us rather than *to* us. The people who are working in schools that fear change more often than not have change imposed on them; people who work in schools that relish change are key participants in that change, own it and understand why it is being made.

Getting it wrong

A headteacher has a crucial role – possibly one of the most crucial roles of all – in putting in place strategies and values that will make schools welcoming of and not resistant to change. School leaders on occasions need to make changes quickly and without consultation but the reality is that most change will need to win over the people affected by the consequences of the change. Getting that simple rule wrong can have rapid and unwelcome repercussions. The example on the following pages illustrates how deceptively easy it is to manage change badly – even when the change is a sensible one. Process is nearly always as important as product and creating a sense that everyone is involved in change management and all views are welcome and considered is an important facet of ensuring change is constructive and effective.

Talking heads

Alison, an experienced primary school headteacher, told us of a change she introduced early into her second headship that did not go as planned:

> I had only been in the school for a couple of weeks but felt reasonably confident because of the fact this was my second headship and I was pretty certain that I knew what I was doing. I noticed that a significant number of children were bringing crisps and sweets in to school in their lunch boxes. I felt very strongly that this was not right and I decided to put an immediate stop to it.
>
> I duly wrote a letter to parents saying that in future all crisps and sweets were banned and that all parents should encourage their sons/daughters to eat fruit as part of their planned diet. In retrospect my passion for good food alongside my conviction that what I was proposing was obviously (in my eyes) eminently sensible and reasonable, made my letter unnecessarily patronising and hectoring in tone. Quite unlike me in fact! The reaction from parents – even those who did not give their children sweets and crisps – was as vigorous as it was unexpected. Some parents actually became quite aggressive because as far as they were concerned they were being lectured to by a somewhat self-righteous individual who had not even had the decency to consult them before making the decision.
>
> In fact, it was the lack of consultation that had angered them much more than the request that they no longer give their children sweets and crisps! I realised very quickly that consultation is essential when introducing change that will affect parents and others in the local community who have dealings with the school. I arranged for a questionnaire to go out retrospectively, got clear support, thank goodness, from the majority of parents and then introduced the no crisps, no sweets rule with no opposition from any quarter. Having to unpick everything in this way was far from ideal however and I made sure that I never made the same mistake again.

Talking heads

Robyn, another primary school head, told us of a change that she believed was introduced well and which continues to impact positively on the culture of the school.

I realised fairly early on in my headship that the school I had come to was viewed as successful and was clearly popular with parents, not least because the results were very good. However, this success came very much at the expense of the children actually enjoying much of what they were doing. I decided that we had to introduce some real quality, excellence and enjoyment into the curriculum and try to get away from the idea that everything we did was first and foremost to achieve some sort of grade. I took the senior leadership team to a school where the curriculum was exciting and enjoyable and they were very impressed.

This started the ball rolling. The key, in my view, was to get my leadership team to choose some area of the curriculum they were comfortable with where they could begin to make the changes I wanted to introduce. They then produced the evidence, were completely won over and almost immediately set out to convince the rest of the staff that making these changes would improve the quality of service we were offering. The fact that they were now promoting it rather than me, made all the difference and the staff bought in to the whole thing.

The reason I think that this change was so successful was more than anything down to the fact that we got everyone to buy in to it first. Of course, the fact that staff, students and parents could appreciate the positive effect it was having on the learning really helped as well!

Bold strokes/long marches

Kanter et al (1992) made the observation that leaders have to balance the demands of 'bold strokes' (immediate decisive actions) with 'long marches' (the overall development of an organisation) effectively. Managing change requires exactly the same degree of sensitivity and judgement. We have already talked about the importance of timing when making changes and the need for judging when a change needs to be made quickly or much more gradually. In both instances we have stressed the importance of winning over the hearts and minds of the recipients of change.

Bold strokes

As for bold strokes, I have already included examples in this chapter where headteachers have been very bold indeed and made unilateral changes quickly and decisively – almost always because they have encountered practices and procedures which they simply could and would not tolerate at any cost.

Sometimes these changes will be accepted more than anything because the head's passion and conviction have been so impressive and convincing. On other occasions there is an element of luck (the example quoted earlier about school bells). There is also the priceless ability to be able to introduce a change quickly that will be accepted equally quickly by everybody because the head has read the situation exactly right – as the following exemplifies.

Talking heads

Elliot, the long serving head of a school in the South West, talked about how he introduced the new teaching and learning responsibilities (TLRs) into his school.

I was very aware how lucky I was to have such a superb staff. And that wasn't just my view. Over the previous 12 years we had had three Ofsted inspections and had been judged outstanding in all of them. Morale was high and the mood around the place was buoyant and upbeat. The new TLR structure was a directive from central government and could not be sidetracked. The legislation allowed for heads to change the staffing structure of the school and, talking to other heads, it was clear that they were going to use this as an opportunity to settle a few scores with some of their teachers who had been a thorn in their sides for some time. I knew that some of my headteacher colleagues were spending days locked in their offices designing complex and, in some cases, quite draconian structures to make sure that they sorted things out once and for all and dealt with what they perceived to be previously unwinnable staffing issues.

I felt uncomfortable about all this for a number of reasons, not least the fact that at my school we resolved issues of underperformance, we didn't duck them. I was also very happy with the existing structure and I knew that the talented motivated staff I had at the school would not welcome and did not deserve any move on my part that appeared to question or devalue the quality of what they were doing.

As it turned out, I called a staff meeting the following day, talked through the structure with them (which in essence was virtually the same as the existing one) and made it clear that on my watch nobody would be financially disadvantaged. In fact, most people came out of it better off. I instinctively knew that this was the right thing to do and events proved that to be true. The problems some of my colleagues in other schools had with their new structures were immense and the resulting discord terribly damaging.

During the conversations I have had with headteachers, the distinction between 'bold strokes' and 'long marches' has been quite striking. Andrew, a seasoned head of three very different schools, said that he took over a school in special measures and decided from the outset that he would have to make changes very quickly and accept no opposition:

You have to take as many people with you as you can but you simply do not have the time to win over all hearts and minds – particularly those who do not want to be won over. I made the commitment that we would go from special measures to specialist status in one year so when we decided on a change, we made the change and dealt with any fall-out. Some were pretty fundamental, like changing the pastoral structure from houses to year groups at a stroke because I knew that to improve rapidly, each year group had a specific contribution to make. When you making changes at this speed and of this significance, you do have to cover all the angles, put the hours in and decide whether any resistance you are getting is justified or just resistance to change per se.

Talking heads

Ann talked about the challenges she faced taking on a coasting comprehensive in the north of England:

When I arrived at the school I could tell that it was good but simply nowhere near as good as it could be. Everybody was very nice and welcoming but they'd lost sight of the fact that they were there to serve the kids. I set out to restructure the staff straightaway and was hit with a barrage of tears and tantrums. I had completely underestimated how upsetting certain members of staff could have such a massively negative influence on the whole school. People went behind my back. The governors were clearly resistant to change and those middle leaders who had been over-promoted to positions they were totally incapable of occupying became very confrontational and destructive.

I knew I was running the real danger of alienating the staff and governors and losing more than I was ever likely to gain from introducing these changes if I didn't communicate the vision clearly and convince a significant minority of the staff that we had far more to lose if we did not radically change the way we approached teaching and learning. Fortunately, I did manage to convince enough key staff, including my leadership team, that we needed to do this and when we saw how everything seemed to improve quite quickly, more and more people were won over. But it was a very close run thing!

Change that really challenges you

Change at any time can be difficult and emotionally draining. Major changes introduced quickly can be particularly demanding and draining on a head's personal resilience and integrity.

Long marches

Planning and implementing more fundamental changes to an organisation requires real skill and is linked to an awareness of how that particular organisation operates – its strengths and weaknesses, the key players, the major obstacles and how to overcome them. If you get any of this wrong you can create major problems and significantly damage your own credibility. You can marginalise key players in the school, and lose sight of the day job, by becoming so immersed in the changes you are looking to effect, and as a result become far less effective in carrying out all those implicit tasks of headship (for example, corridor conversations, saying thanks, asking after people's problems, talking to students!) that are such an integral part of the role.

Positive, successful long-term change nearly always follows the same pattern, as shown in the table below.

Nine Step Model for Making Sustainable Change

Step	Action
Step 1	Identify the need
Step 2	Audit the current strengths, weaknesses, opportunities and threats (SWOT analysis) relating to that need
Step 3	Consult widely, equitably, appropriately and intelligently
Step 4	Plan the change very carefully
Step 5	Advertise, explain, communicate and justify the change
Step 6	Implement the change
Step 7	Manage the processes required for the change to 'bed down'
Step 8	Monitor and evaluate the change
Step 9	Make the necessary refinements

Nobody would claim that any one of these stages is especially revolutionary or controversial but it is so easy to get some or all of them wrong! One of the real dangers is missing the final stage and omitting to put in place proper and robust mechanisms to evaluate the quality and success of the innovation that has been introduced. It is deceptively easy as a head to introduce a change that you think is absolutely essential and then never allow any opposition to it. Indeed, the extent to which you can quite belligerently continue to hold on to views that have become outdated prejudices, without you ever acknowledging it, can be very destructive. That is when you need honesty from your leadership team!

I really am not prejudiced at all!

I vividly remember working with a head I admired greatly who had no time for faculty structures and would not countenance job descriptions of any kind. As a direct result of his conviction, I held on to the same view for the first ten years of my headship until I had to be strongly advised by a trusted member of his leadership team that I had to modify my views because the size and complexity of the school I was now running could not operate efficiently unless clear job specifications were introduced and we moved over to a faculty structure.

Schools that manage change tend to be entrepreneurial in tone; those that do not, tend to be prescriptive and bureaucratic. To ensure that transformational change works well you need to capture the mindsets of the people engaged in the change. If you are really good at managing change, those involved will end up thinking that they managed the change themselves, which is a great result because it means they value and embrace what is being introduced and will therefore support and defend it. That last part is crucial because experienced heads know that some teachers can be brilliant at nodding through changes in public that they have no intention of implementing behind closed doors!

Conclusion

As noted earlier, much of the thinking that governs making change work is rooted in common sense. However, there can be so many occasions in the course of a school year when common sense appears to be very uncommon indeed. Themes coming out of the interviews with headteachers reflect a considerable degree of agreement about what works and what does not work when you are looking to implement change. Another clear theme of this chapter was the distinction between changes that are made quickly and decisively and those that are much more planned, protracted and thought through.

However, the heads interviewed for this book all emphasised how important it was to make sure that changes actually improve things and how dangerous and damaging it is if you as a leader end up unintentionally introducing something that reduces rather than enhances the quality that was already there. All the heads also stressed how crucially important this area of their work was. If you get it wrong, you create all sorts of problems for you and your school. Get it right and it can make a huge difference to your own reputation (if that is important to you!) and the quality of service you are offering the students.

Action points

- You have to put in place the structure and culture to recognise the need for change and then put in place the right means to secure it. No mean feat!

- As a headteacher you have to create a climate where the right changes are made at the right time by the right people. Again, this is a real challenge but nonetheless a fundamental responsibility for school leaders.

- The key to effective change is the free flow of information (both ways) and the sharing of responsibilities. If you fail to achieve that you will fail to achieve much at all.

- Never lose sight of the fact that introducing a change successfully is only one part of the process. You must have rigorous processes in place that will challenge that change and be prepared to change again if that is what is required.

- Put the following quote up on your office wall: 'We cannot re-structure a structure that is splintered at its roots. Adding wings to caterpillars does not create butterflies – it creates dysfunctional caterpillars. Butterflies are created through transformation'.

- Don't be defensive if people challenge a change you have personally introduced. It may well need to be challenged and the fact that people are prepared to do so says a lot of positive things about your leadership style. Furthermore, ask yourself whether it is time for that change to be changed!

- Don't be afraid of change – embrace it as an inevitable and integral part of the improvement agenda. Keep at the centre of your thinking the mantra we quote in the chapter that 'For everything to remain the same, everything must change'. It will prevent you from becoming complacent!'

9 Next steps: moving on or moving out?

Chapter overview

The main areas covered in this chapter include:

- The advantages, challenges and drawbacks of second and third headships.
- How to make your exit as painless and graceful as possible.
- Life after headship: the options and implications.
- Deciding when is the best time to leave your school.
- Learning from mistakes: what essential truths, pieces of wisdom would be of value to incoming headteachers?

Second, third, fourth headships?

Several of my interviewees for this book had more than one headship. Chris, the head of a secondary school in Gloucestershire that had recently achieved an outstanding Ofsted report remembered his first headship and how markedly different it was from his current one.

> I found my first headship extremely difficult and demanding from day one and to be honest it never felt any different from the day I started to the day I finished. The leadership team, two of whom had applied unsuccessfully for the headship, was completely out of touch and showed from the beginning of my time there that they felt no need to give me any support or loyalty.
>
> The culture of the school was centred on the philosophy that mediocrity was inevitable, in view of the catchment area and the type of students the school attracted, and survival was about the best any teacher could aspire to. I spent four intensely unrewarding and unproductive years there and came close to leaving

teaching altogether. When I came to this [new] school I could not believe the difference. I enjoyed the challenge it from the minute I walked in the front door and I still enjoy it today.

Headship and context are discussed in Chapter 10 but Chris's experience of two quite different schools with very different sets of expectations shows how deceptively easy it is to assume that just because you have been unsuccessful in one school, you cannot be successful in another. It can of course work in reverse too: a number of high-profile headteachers have moved from one post where they had achieved great things to a school where everything has gone horribly wrong.

This can have an absolutely devastating effect on the individual concerned, sometimes one from which they never recover. The possible move, therefore, from first to second headship needs to be very carefully thought through; those headteachers who assume that if they have been successful in one school they will automatically be successful in another need to step back and reflect on the real challenges that second and subsequent headships will throw up.

Talking heads

Philip, the head of a large mixed secondary school in Norfolk, spoke to us about his decision to go for a second headship:

All logic told me that I was mad to consider leaving my first school. My children were still of compulsory school age and had no desire to move out of the area. Moving house is expensive and we really liked where we lived. However, at 48, I was conscious that I would soon have no choice in the matter. I was acutely aware that my school was at the end of an era and I no longer had the energy or the interest to take it into its next phase. Deep down I knew I had to uproot!

Listening to my friends and discussing the issue at length with my wife, I decided to look for another school in a very specific area of the country and then see what happened. As fate would have it, the next week the ideal school in the right area appeared in the Times Educational Supplement. I applied for the post and got the job. It happened so quickly it hardly gave me any time to consider whether or not I was doing the right thing but in reality I knew I was.

> Beginning my second headship was such a huge contrast to beginning my first. I felt from the start the real benefits of already having done the job. I also felt that completing my MBA had given me invaluable additional experience. This time I was conscious of moving straight into a role which I knew and understood and having the confidence and clarity of thought from the outset. I also felt I was able to move straight to the central issues and confident enough to embrace colleagues and ensure they were involved in consultation, decision making and putting ideas into action. So now, one year into my second headship I'm certain it was the right move for me and, thankfully for my family. The very different context has given me renewed interest and energy for work.

Philip's confidence about second headships is not shared by everyone who takes up this option. Some heads will say that they feel more nervous about their second and third headships than they did about their first, citing as one of the major causes of their apprehension the fact that, having done it once, they know how much factors outside their control can impact on their ability to make things happen. They will also remember how, occasionally, things worked out well more by luck than judgement and that innovations that were very successful in their first school could be anything but in their second.

However, the increased confidence that Philip mentions about taking on a second headship is true. You may not realise it, but having gone through the experience of being a head, you will be in a much stronger position to see what needs to be done in subsequent headships and how best to make things happen. If you have had a successful first headship, your implicit confidence in your own ability to do the job, even though you think you are not confident at all, will be clear to those working with you.

Some heads have entertained the prospect of second headships to the extent that they have applied and been shortlisted for jobs and then withdrawn at the eleventh hour because they have realised very forcibly that they do not wish to repeat the challenges, successes and disappointments of their first headship. 'Why repeat what I have already done – what's the point in doing that?' is the question they ask themselves and one that they frequently cannot find a convincing answer to.

The key word here is 'repeat'. When looking to move to second headships it is wise to make certain that the new school is very different from your first, in order to make sure that the key objectives will be different. A classic example would be to move from a very poor-performing school in a challenging, deprived area to a high-achieving school in the leafy suburbs because the challenge of moving an organisation from bad to good is very different from moving a school from very good to even better!

Talking heads

Rosemary is currently on her third headship. Here she talks about what it is like to move on from one headship to another, and then another!

When asked to reflect on my third headship, I was tempted to reply flippantly 'maybe third time lucky'. I remembered the salutary conclusion of research: just because you are a successful head in one school does not necessarily mean you will be successful in another school. Some skills are transferable, but every school, every staff, is different and different cultures, different circumstances inevitably lead to new challenges. I still suffer from what can be termed educational or headship paranoia – that even after ten years as a headteacher and in my third school, someone will find me out and realise that I don't really know what I'm doing!

In my first headship it was not possible to visit the new school a great deal but in my second and third headships I managed to interview all the staff before I arrived. This meant I was able to make initial acquaintances, put names to faces and ask them to write about their present post and future aspirations and what they considered to be the strengths and weaknesses of the school. This gave me a fascinating (though not necessarily fully accurate!) insight into the school. The fact I was not yet in post meant that there was a neutrality about the discussions which I felt allowed people to be more honest and open than they might otherwise have been.

I'm not sure I would have had the confidence to do that in my first headship but I'm so glad I did. I still feel I make too many mistakes but I'm very aware that ten years in headship has taught me that I'm still learning the skills of headship and will I hope continue to do so until the day I walk away from the job. Doing a third headship had strengthened my conviction that it's essential to retain the vision, the enthusiasm and the buzz if only for one's own satisfaction.

As with so much to do with headship however, there are no hard and fast rules about first, second, third and even fourth headships (and I do know of one head in north London who is on his seventh headship!). Nowadays, of course, with the role of head as chief executive becoming more and more familiar, successful headteachers can remain in post and increase their sphere of influence, at least in the UK, by opening academies, heading up federations and taking over other schools, thereby rendering irrelevant the question of whether or not to take on additional headships.

However, the evidence would suggest that most people who move on to new headships enjoy the experience and the schools they join benefit from the fact that their new head has already done the job before. It is vitally important that all heads who are contemplating such a move do everything they can to make sure that such a major change turns out to be a change for the better and not for the worse. It is so important to consider all the options very carefully and not to be persuaded by what can sometimes be the superficial gloss of 'greener grass'. People's careers and school reputations have been shattered by not getting this right.

Life after headship: moving on

Much of this book as was made clear from the outset, centres on personal opinions and truths drawn from the experiences of people actually doing the job of headship, as opposed to reading or theorising about it. As you know, there is a tremendous amount of literature interpreting, analysing and dissecting the role of headship and yet there is far less on what to do when you finally leave the job. However, the more you talk to practising heads, especially (and understandably) those in the twilight of their careers, the more you realise how much it concentrates the mind and how daunting the prospect can be for many headteachers. There is no doubt in my mind that the challenge of managing life after headship is real and tough and needs to be very carefully planned.

An important factor that has significantly influenced those who are considering moving out of headship and taking on new roles is the (worldwide) recession. It was generally agreed, prior to the financial meltdown that began in 2008, that school leaders in many countries, including the UK, could earn a very healthy living from consultancy work after they gave up headship. Most heads would have a shelf life of at least two years after leaving school where they could, for example, command very high salaries for advisory support, school improvement, performance assessment and management, financial expertise, work in international schools as inspectors or take up roles in regional or central government.

However, there is increasing evidence that this source of income is drying up – a fact that makes taking early retirement for some much less attractive.

Deciding when to leave: how to exit gracefully

Leaving early

Over the past 20 years a significant number of the heads I have known have taken early retirement and/or moved from headship to another role – and it is almost always something to do with education. There are any number of different reasons and motives for leaving headship early. Some people find that the stress of the job finally becomes too invasive and counter-productive. Some decide that the accountability and responsibility of the job becomes too much – a trend that has increased dramatically over the last 15 years and frequently results in heads taking early retirement. Others just run out of steam and enthusiasm and realise that they can no longer give as much as they need to if they are going to manage the role effectively and well.

Of course, the reasons are not always negative. I know of several heads (including David Middlewood) who left successful headships and found new jobs so stimulating that they never returned. However, whatever the reason, moving on to a new position necessarily requires you to adjust your sights, your expectations and your responsibilities.

Pause for thought

- As a headteacher you are comfortable with and have become very used to being in charge. It is hard when you are no longer in that position. Just imagine how frustrating it is to be in a badly chaired meeting for the first time!
- It is more than likely that your new job will have few if any of the impressive networks of support structures that nearly always come with headship.
- Many bosses do of course have secretaries but it is likely that they will do much more of their own administration than many heads as a rule do. Heads who have gone into consultancy work often say how much they took these support networks for granted when they were heads and how much they miss them!

Talking heads

Daniela left her job as head of a special school to become a university tutor. A year into post, she reflected on how it has changed her and refined her perceptions of her headship:

> There is an enormous cultural difference between working in a school and working in a university. I am still beguiled by the air of calm that generally prevails. This is not to say that the department does not have its fair share of crises and panics but the response is different: I sense a tangible air of thoughtful reflection, which is in stark contrast to the suppressed panic to be found in other sectors of the education system. Adapting to this change of culture has been very difficult, involving as it does, a loss of personal control. As a head, you feel responsible for everything and to find yourself in a place where you are no longer the lynchpin is very scary at first!
>
> After almost a full year in the job, I like it more and more but I have had to adapt to a completely different way of working, not to mention a huge drop in salary! I still find it difficult to accept that I am no longer in charge. I do have delegated responsibilities but I am not the ultimate buck stopper. Can you imagine how that feels? Well, actually it felt strangely liberating at first and yet not quite right. Nobody asked me to solve any major problems!
>
> Another aspect of the job that took some getting used to was having to organise my own working time. You may say that headteachers do that all the time. Well, with the benefit of hindsight, let me tell you that they do not! As a head, you are out the beck and call of everybody, all the time. There is no time when you are not thinking about work and during the day I realise now how often I was being sent to places or people (frequently by my secretary) because that's what was needed at the time. Life now is so different!

There are no hard and fast rules about when to leave a school and move on to something else or when to retire. There used to be pockets of received wisdom about when a headteacher should change course and do something else. Many commentators would suggest that five to seven years is the optimum time span to stay in one school because it was felt that after seven years a headteacher is likely to become bored or disengaged or too set in his/her ways to be truly effective any longer.

It is certainly true that after about seven years it is much more likely that your leadership team and your governors will have developed a very clear idea of what you will and will not tolerate and they will have accepted that here are certain no-go areas that they will no longer venture into. And that is dangerous. In Chapter 8, I mention the implicit dangers of openly parading your prejudices while at the same time failing to recognise them as such and consequently brooking no argument that challenges them. Such an approach will undoubtedly render you much less open to constructive argument and much less effective as a consequence.

In recent years the idea of the 'seven year itch' in headship has been challenged. Researchers, Woods (2002) for example, have suggested that heads who are comfortable and challenged in their roles and who work in a school that fits them and their style of leadership become increasingly effective the longer they stay in post, even into their sixties. They only cease to be effective when they themselves no longer enjoy the job and many heads will work for more than 20 years in the same school before they reach that stage. However, all heads will feel differently about their work and will have different reasons and motives for leaving to move on to something else.

In my view, the golden rule is to make sure that you, as the head, leave your school before other people – your leadership team, your chair of governors for example – gently suggest that it might be a good idea. A good rule of thumb is to leave when you think you still have one good year left in you and not some time after you have already completed it. In my opinion, most headteachers will instinctively know when it is time to leave. Several of my interviewees have talked about the nagging little voice in their head that becomes increasingly strident after each term. My advice would be that as soon as you hear that voice listen to it, waste no time and take action!

Moving out

It is not surprising to find that there is comparatively little literature or research into the very particular challenges of planning and moving into retirement. Yet the reality is that retiring from headship takes almost as much thought and courage in my view as deciding to take the job in the first place. Of course, most books on leadership will be read by people who are new to the role or who are well established and looking to improve their practice. It is unlikely that a book on leadership that takes as its main theme the challenges of retirement and targets school leaders in their late fifties and sixties would be a runaway success. Yet there is a real need for guidance and good sense from those who have managed the transition successfully because headteachers, generally by their very nature, are not good at thinking deeply about their own needs and planning what to do when they finish.

Pause for thought

- Remember how important it is to leave gracefully and with your personal and professional dignity intact.
- Do whatever you need to do to make sure that the transition process for the incoming head is as seamless and productive as it can be. Your own feelings have to be put on the back burner!
- Accept the fact, however hard, that as soon as you leave no matter how wonderful, charismatic, popular and effective you have been as a head, your school will move on. If you have done your job well it will move on to bigger and better things, which is how it should be.

Leaving a job to take on another headship, for example, is very different from leaving a job for retirement. Although you may be sad to leave your current post, you are inevitably excited and apprehensive about new challenges at your new post and much of your time and thought will be given over to that. Leaving to move into retirement is very different and no one can be prepared for the number of powerful and unsettling emotions that it generates. You are, after all, not just giving up a job, you are giving up a way of life that has for a very long time consumed much of your waking hours.

Talking heads

Sarah, the head of a medium sized 11–16 secondary school in the West Midlands, talks candidly about how difficult she found handing her school over to someone else:

> I was quite unprepared for how threatened and out of sorts I felt about the whole process. Even though I was absolutely certain that I was doing the

right thing in retiring and leaving my headship after 17 years at the school, I could not have anticipated how I would feel after I had told the chair of governors, he had announced it to the full governing body and then I had told staff the following day. Even though people were very nice to me – full of sympathy (one or two actually asked me to re-consider, which was nice) and supposed envy that I was moving on to a life of leisure, I could not believe how quickly the organisation moved into 'finding a replacement mode'.

Friends had warned me that as soon as I had made my intention to retire public I would be, as one put it, 'a busted flush'. Nevertheless I could not apprehend or indeed accept the realisation that my views were no longer valid and that any plans I might have had for the remaining few months in post would have to be shelved or forgotten in case they did not match with my successor's. Never has the expression 'The King is dead, long live the King' been more apt or stark. People were listening to me as usual but they were not *really* listening! Quite understandably, their efforts and attention were being targeted at finding a new head which, although absolutely necessary and obvious, was something I found terribly difficult to deal with. And I felt such a fool for feeling like that!

Having now gone through the process and come out the other side relatively unscathed, I realise why some heads talk about leaving their schools as being akin to dealing with grief. Whether it's the fear of the unknown or loss of status and importance (after all, you have been in charge for such a long time!), I do not know but it caught me totally unaware. I was extremely fortunate that the person appointed to take over from me was someone I really liked and respected. He was also very sensitive, understanding, instinctively aware of what I was going through and keen to pick my brains as much as he could before taking up post. That made all the difference.

Significant change

In the first decade of this century the economic situation across Europe has changed dramatically in the light of the anticipated change to teachers' pensions which will significantly reduce their value and the fact that the retirement age is going to rise to 67. Recently I met Peter, who was a headteacher of a federation of primary schools. He told me that even though he was still in his late thirties he had already been a head for ten years. Peter was now facing what he considered to be the daunting prospect of being a headteacher for another 28 years. He told me that, whatever happened, there was no way he was going to do the job in his fifties. It seems highly likely that many headteachers, even if they do multiple headships will, like Peter, now be looking to leave headship and pursue other avenues some time before their retirement. Even retirees at 67 can expect, if current trends continue, to be retired for at least 20 years.

Headship by its very nature is almost certainly not good preparation for retirement. Frequently, people who are in jobs that do not stimulate them or give them any sense of vocation or job satisfaction compensate for the fact by developing healthy social networks and taking up hobbies that engage their interest in a way their day job never can. Headship, however, presents consistent and unfair demands on your time if you are really committed to it. It can take over your life if you let it and it will consume pretty much every waking day. Gronn (2003: 153) describes being a headteacher as being one of the 'greedy' occupations. He says the work becomes 'the measure of what one is and not just what one does' so that 'one lives to work, rather than works to live'.

It is also a very people-centred role, which means that as a headteacher you are, for much of the working week, constantly interacting with people. Many of the heads I have interviewed openly admit that this feature of the job makes them fairly anti-social in their private lives. One of my interviewees was articulating a view echoed by many other headteachers when she said that, in view of the fact that she spent all and every day meeting and talking to people, the last thing she wanted to do when she got home was to go out and socialise. Another problem is that in the light of how all-consuming the role is and how involving it can be, many headteachers have neither the will nor the energy to take up hobbies or other pastimes that will give them another perspective on how to use their time as a possible outlet for their energies when they have retired.

Of course I am well aware that I am making what could be seen as sweeping generalisations here and that many heads will protest that they have plenty of spare time, lots of hobbies and a vibrant social life; nevertheless, I still think it important to voice a real issue about the uneasy relationship between being a school leader and moving into retirement. I also believe that any thoughtful headteacher, even if he or she is many years away from leaving the job behind allows sufficient time, thought and energy over a sustained period as to how retirement is going to be managed effectively and successfully.

For just over five years (1999–2005) David and I co-edited *Headship Matters* (Optimus) which came out six times a year and featured a wide range of articles on school leadership. I am pleased now on refection that we included a number of contributions on life after headship which included some pieces on moving into retirement. They resonate with me much more now than at the time we were publishing the magazine and I make no apology for sharing some of the content with you here.

Talking heads

Andy, an extremely successful and highly-regarded headteacher in the West Country, reflected on how he was looking to move into retirement:

Even in the preparation for going, there can be no slowing. But I am beginning to peer into the unknown, seeking a passage into phase three that will give me some of the satisfaction of the past 37 years without the killing pace. I know for certain that my future will not be Ofsted driven. The idea of being involved in Threshold Assessment or becoming a performance management guru must be akin to selling my soul for 30 pieces of silver and the government's model of stepping down for headteachers to become classroom teachers is plainly daft.

I dream of opportunities to go into a school community and to work alongside the school leadership team as they seek to improve their school still further. The role of a listening and sometimes questioning friend, the mentoring role, is sadly neglected in educational practice. It might not work, I might have nothing to give, but the thought of working flat out until the end of the year and then switching off the tap of all my educational energies seems such a waste.

Whatever the future, the past and present have been and remain a great privilege. In schools we may not have the immediate impact of the surgeon or give the heights of collective pleasure or anguish of a Premier League footballer, opera singer or ballet dancer, but we uniquely develop the minds and values of those who will one day become the leaders of those generations that we will never know. At the moment that thought must suffice as I prepare for my last summer term.

Another contribution came from Brian, a headteacher who has now been happily retired for several years. In his article he presented some general 'rules' or pieces of advice he would like to pass on to those about to retire. I believe his thoughts are worth sharing:

1   Amend your way of life. When you leave your school resist all temptations to return: no going back to give out prizes or attend concerts. This is the secret of happiness.

2   Get a financial adviser to help you think about money and order your needs and priorities. Get used to the idea of spending money now rather than saving it for a rainy day!

3   Make sure you acquire the habit of daily exercise. If you have not been a regular exerciser you will be amazed how your health and general feeling of well-being will improve.

4   Have at least one objective interest. It could be painting, military history, beekeeping, anything that has an existence of its own and isn't anything to do with you so that when you are doing it you are taken out of yourself.

5   Learn something. You have been promoting learning in others all your working life so now go and do some of your own. There is beauty, fun and pleasure in acquiring new skills.

6   Cultivate acquaintances. It is so rewarding to find after years as a head, defined by the sound of grinding axes, that there are people who are disinterestedly friendly and value your company and your good will for its own sake.

7   Do some good works. By giving assistance you will feel as though you still have a contribution to make and you will feel the great satisfaction of being valued for your help, rather than being toadied to for what you can bestow.

8   Get used to and make the most of having more time. Heads work to tight schedules but from now on you can slow down to whatever pace you please. Note however that it takes a long time – perhaps as much as a year or more – to learn how to do this and to get the 100 miles an hour lifestyle out of your system.

9   Remember that one of the great unforeseen delightful surprises of retirement is the sheer pleasure of being able to do what you like, and if you don't like doing it, stopping that and doing something else.

The value of listing Brian's thoughts here is that they illustrate how utterly different being retired is from working as a headteacher and that the personal and professional adjustment required is significant. Unlike most other jobs, headteachers cannot really ease themselves into retirement: one headteacher reflected on the fact that there are few if any jobs where a person can retire from being a leader with such wide-ranging responsibilities and status on the Friday and be painting the garden fence on the Monday. This is why it can be tough.

The reassuring signs are, however, that most headteachers enjoy their retirement and handle it well in their own particular ways. I know of some school leaders who after headship plunge into charity work abroad or study for doctorates in American universities or are driven to acquire new leadership skills and move into other businesses. Others are quite happy to do the gardening, meet friends for lunch and take up sculpture. In the end it is down to personal preference to make sure that when you do retire it works for you.

Pause for thought

- Even if you are still some way off retirement age, remember how quickly time flies!
- If and when you leave headship, try to avoid replicating the special sense of achievement and satisfaction that so often comes with headship. It has been mentioned several times in the book that the role is unique so attempting to replicate it in a different context is never going to work.
- Enjoy the positive benefits of no longer doing the job. For many, the loss of accountability and responsibility is a blessed relief.

Learning from experience

At the end of each interview I conducted with experienced, long-serving headteachers I asked them if they had any major regrets and, with the benefit of hindsight, if there were any essential truths or pieces of wisdom they would want to pass on to new and/or aspiring heads. At this point in the chapter it seems appropriate that I list some of their responses to provide, I hope, some food for thought. They are in no particular order of priority or importance.

- 'Headship is about managing the boundaries. It is about support and learning from one another. Distributed leadership will help develop leadership qualities. And remember, all the time you are in headship, that you are not indispensable!'

- 'Never believe your own publicity. Be true to yourself, stick to your principles, be choosy about the school you choose, build something you can be proud of and enjoy the experience. It's a wonderful job!'

- 'Never worry about appointing people who are cleverer than you. Appoint them and then give them the time and space to make a real contribution to the improvement agenda.'

- 'I would definitely have acted more quickly in my first three years of headship to address under-achievement. I should have gone in straightaway and not been so concerned about people's egos and sensitivities.'

- 'You absolutely know when it's time to leave. Complacency and familiarity begin to creep in and you start to feel curiously detached at school events such as parents' evenings and school concerts.'

- 'I wish I could learn to be more patient and less demanding. I think I've got better but I'm still not great! My naivety has let me down on occasions and I regret the fact that the job has made me harder and more cynical.'

- 'Never forget that teaching will have done more for you that you can ever do for it. It has given me a relentless focus and made me feel needed.'

- 'I wish I'd had the self-discipline to slow down a little and enjoy each term more. I was always looking for the next challenge, the next hurdle, the next set of results etc. I regret that now very much.'

- 'On reflection I wish I'd had closer interpersonal relationships with the kids. I spent too much time doing things for them and not enough time talking to them.'

- 'When all is said and done, headship is about persuading and cajoling lots of different people to head off in the same direction. It's not about banging the table and demanding unswerving obedience.'

Conclusion

I am very aware that of all the chapters in the book, this is by far the most personal: the heads we interviewed spoke candidly about the very particular and sometimes intensely private issues that relate solely and specifically to headship. The only way you can experience the wide range of emotions a headteacher will go through when leaving a school or taking on another one or moving into retirement is to be a headteacher.

No amount of second-guessing or theorising or poring over research findings will accurately recreate the personal and professional hurdles and challenges that have been the subject of this chapter. One of the reasons heads are often dubious about papers presented at conferences on school leadership by people who have never been headteachers is that, until you have done the job, you cannot hope to appreciate how uniquely demanding it is and what special pressures and demands it places on you.

How you deal with the issues raised here will be down to you and the manner in which you manage them and that will very largely depend on who you are as a person – as discussed in Chapter 4. When I was interviewing all the heads for this book the one clear message for me was that there is no proven recipe for successful career development, no right or wrong answers, but nonetheless, when you, as a headteacher, feel instinctively that you need a change of direction or you need to call a halt to whatever you are doing and move on, then, for your sake and for the sanity of all those around you, do it!

Action points

- As a head you probably spend a good deal of time helping other people sort out *their* career plans. Make sure that you find the time and space to sort your own career dilemmas and aspirations out and be methodical and rigorous in how you go about dealing with them.

- Sarah's honest and brave account in this chapter of how hard she found leaving her school will be recognised by many heads who have felt many similar emotions. Be warned and make sure you are prepared for the catalogue of emotions you will experience!

- If you feel the need and have the opportunity to go for a second headship, take it. The evidence is very much on your side that it will be a successful and rewarding career move.

- Even if you are happy in your job, never stop checking the job sections in professional journal. Sometimes, by so doing, feelings that you thought were dormant or non-existent will come to the surface.

- As has already been said in other chapters in this book, make sure you maintain a network of trusted colleagues and friends who will be able to help you make what will be very tough decisions as you progress through headship.

10 Final reflections

Chapter overview

In this final chapter, we reflect on what has emerged from the interviews, discussions, personal recollections and the collected wisdom of the headteachers who have contributed to this book. Topics covered include:

- The place and importance of context and how it impacts on your personal and professional career path.
- Headship and the changing landscape.
- Essential 'truths' about the reality of school leadership.
- Observations/reflections on what makes for an effective school.

School leaders and context

There is a good deal of evidence that, in spite of all the many different kinds and styles of effective leadership that have been identified, the reason it is not possible to pick one as the manifestly obvious 'best' one is because a leader's effectiveness is highly dependent on context. This is sometimes equally obvious in business when a very successful chief executive moves to a different company or even a different sphere of activity and fails. Contexts can be very similar but ultimately each one is unique – rather like people and families! There are different types of schools but within that typology each individual school is special, simply because people are different.

But can a really effective headteacher or principal succeed in any school, whatever its environment and context? If you have all the right attributes, skills and talents, are they transferable with you wherever you take them and therefore can you use them equally effectively in whatever school you lead? The two authors of this chapter have always been clear that they believed they were effective in specific ways but that there were a number of types of schools that they would not necessarily have succeeded in. The way to deal with this in the UK's system was simple – do not apply for such schools! In countries where the leadership posts are allocated centrally, such restrictions are considered by the allocating body, although we are not aware of any research that explores the success or otherwise of the two systems in this respect.

It has to be admitted that not all of the leaders interviewed by Richard for this book had these reservations. A small number were confident that they could have succeeded in any school, regardless of type or environment; significantly more acknowledged that there were schools they would almost certainly fail in. They felt they had sufficient skills and commitment and, above all, the adaptability to apply their talents to the needs of any school.

It is interesting to reflect on a few of the issues that might influence any potential leaders as to which schools they might be most suited, for example, the following values:

- If you passionately believe in co-educational schooling, could you successfully lead a single-sex school? Or vice versa?
- If you passionately believe in all-ability schooling, could you successfully lead a selective school?
- If you strongly oppose fee-paying schooling, could you lead a private school?
- If you have no strong religious faith, could you lead a faith school?

And there are other values which are relevant, in terms of political belief, social justice, and such which might play a part.

As for the socio-economic environment, the range of contexts can be huge – from leafy green prosperous settings to seriously impoverished inner city contexts, but you must remember that *all* children have the same right to an effective education where effective leadership is needed. Given that, is it a question of 'horses for courses' or are there school leaders who could succeed in any or all of these contexts?

What is not in dispute perhaps is that the leadership style would need to be significantly different in these different contexts if you are to succeed. How does this sit with the exhortation in Chapter 4 that you need to develop your own style? We believe that underpinning your own leadership style, which you learn through experience – including perhaps trial and error – are the personal values that make you the person you are. Values were identified in Chapter 1 as part of effective leadership across all fields, including business and industry, and in considering the issue of context they become overtly crucial.

We know of one highly effective deputy head, passionately committed to comprehensive education as a means of helping deprived children to achieve their potential. Determined to gain a headship 'at any price', he applied for many posts only to be regularly rejected. Eventually, he gained a headship in a deeply disadvantaged and impoverished school in a city in a run-down area, where unemployment was very high and criminal activity, involving drugs, was widespread. The daily task was horrendous – with break-ins, vandalism, hostile parents, un-cooperative staff, poor resourcing, an unhelpful local authority – and eventually he took early retirement though ill-health.

Perhaps another person might have succeeded, but he was defeated by the context and so a valuable person with clear educational principles and commitment who would undoubtedly been a highly-effective leader was lost to the system. His personal values were right; the context was wrong for him. His leadership style, which was essentially collaborative, was perhaps not suitable for such a 'tough' context. Possibly a more authoritative style was needed in that setting and there are people who can effortlessly move between such styles according to the context, without sacrificing their personal values. It is not at all easy, however.

What defeated this leader were the specific aspects of the relentless daily routine and, as outlined in Chapter 1, constantly dealing with the day-to-day mix of people, events, questions, concerns and problems is one of the things that makes school leadership special. Thus, as each context is unique, so it becomes critically important for leaders to know their own leadership style, understand what works for them, and remain true to their values – above all, focusing on what is likely to be best for the children and young people in that particular context.

The changing landscape?

Looking into the future is always a precarious business, but anyone who is considering a school leadership role needs to be aware of the possible scenarios that will exist in the job they will do. They can then take these into account, weighing up the pros and cons, helping them to decide if that is what they want.

In developed countries, certainly in Western ones, the trend towards increased autonomy for individual institutions is almost certain to continue. Even in post-Soviet new republics, there is evidence of a trend towards more institution-based management (Bush 2008). While this growing autonomy will continue to increase the authority and responsibility of school leaders, it will simultaneously increase the pressures and, significantly, the accountability of the post.

What is not clear is the extent to which that accountability will be exercised at national, local or institutional level. Who will act when the autonomous school is deemed to be under performing? A further question to consider is the level at which the training and preparation for school leaders will be provided. A feature that seems certain to remain is that schools will work together in more and more ways – families, clusters, federations. These liaisons will take many forms but the willingness and ability to form such partnerships will be key to a future leader's effectiveness.

A third element is surely the growing involvement and key part that schools will play in community transformation as they become more and more important in the social justice agenda that they will be part of. While initiatives such as 'No Child Left Behind' (US) and 'Every Child Matters' (England and Wales) fade from the headlines while other government policies dominate, what they represent is too powerful to be lost and we are confident that their concerns will be even more central as this century proceeds. Linked with this community interaction, as pressures on our environment increase alarmingly, the need for schools to recognise and insist on the sustainability of their work can only become more important, as it will in all organisations (see Chapter 1).

This list cannot be exhaustive but it may give an indication of some of what future school leaders may need to consider. Chapters 2 to 9 of this book have given a frank view of the reality of being a school leader and how to cope with this reality. As the book makes clear, there is no one 'magic' recipe, no single way that guarantees success; however, it has stressed that the key to doing a good job and serving the people you work for well, is perhaps to know yourself and then *be* yourself as much as is humanly possible while carrying out the job. Some of the qualities and skills we feel are needed for successful leadership and management of extended schools are: 'risk-taking, radical thinking, entrepreneurialism, dogged determination, passion for learning, belief in dynamic partnerships,' (Middlewood and Parker, 2009: 152). But perhaps the most important thing for successful headteachers and principals looking back on their working lives is that they remained true to their principles and beliefs

Essential 'truths' about school leadership

A key objective of this book has, of course, been to attempt to capture at least some of what we describe as the 'reality of school leadership'. A major problem is that one person's reality could be another person's fantasy, just as one headteacher's truth might well be another headteacher's heresy. That being said, we asked all of our interviewee headteachers if they could make one observation that they considered represented an essential truth of headship based on their own experience of the role. We include some of their responses here in the hope that they may provide some food for thought and reflection.

- 'Never forget how easy it is to be sidetracked, to let things slide and begin to accept inferiority. Hold on to your intuition, listen to wise mentors, stick to your agenda.'

- 'I know I could never be successful or fulfilled in a school that did not have a defining characteristic. It is never a good idea to accept a headship just because it is a headship.'

- 'Don't water the rocks. You will never convince some people to give you the loyalty and support you need. Concentrate on those who do and don't waste your energy on those who never will.'

- 'Accept the fact that there are always going to be times when you doubt yourself and your ability to make things happen – particularly when the going gets tough. Perseverance and bloody-mindedness can be great friends at times like this!'

- 'Remember that people will be very reasonable about your mistakes if you are honest about them. But try very hard to learn every lesson that every mistake will present.'

- 'It is so important to enjoy each job for its own sake and take up every opportunity before you reach headship. The people who seem most disaffected as heads always seem to me to be the ones who were concentrating too much on the destination and not enough on the journey.'

- 'Be true to yourself and, whatever else you do, never start believing in your own legend.'

- 'Remember that nothing prepares you for your first headship; everyone experiences the 'rabbit in the headlights' syndrome and if people say otherwise they are lying!'

In all the interviews carried out with headteachers – who were clearly talented professionals with their own personalities and their own agendas – it was heartening to see significant measure of agreement emerge from these school leaders about what they considered to be school leaders' key roles and responsibilities and what it takes to effect transformational leadership. I found myself agreeing with so much of what they said about why headship is so all-consuming and empowering (if you get it right) and was encouraged by the fact that whatever new initiative, proposals or government policies come into play, the best headteachers will always be looking to put the needs and aspirations of their learners at the centre of everything they do.

Interviewing the headteachers for this book has also reaffirmed how crucially important the headteacher is in developing and defining the educational philosophy of his or her school. Of course, there are aspects of a school's character that school leaders can have little or no influence over but the learning culture of the school will, more than anything else, reflect their own particular passions and pedagogical convictions. A combination of our own experiences and the views of the headteachers interviewed leads us to propose certain fundamental truths about what we believe makes for a good school.

- First and most foremost, the quality of the relationships between teacher and learner, created and fostered by outstanding leadership, is crucially important in determining whether schools succeed or fail.

- Secondly, all those involved in teaching and learning should be allowed the freedom and flexibility to make sure that learning is real, life-long, exciting, challenging and enriching. School leaders should resist any and all attempts to reduce education and the role of schools to learning by numbers or allow themselves to be governed by ill-informed opinions based on consensus rather than evidence.

- Thirdly, there should be no arbitrary barriers placed on who learns and who teaches. We should always be looking to learn from each other and anyone who tries to regulate and restrict teaching to those who have the 'right' qualifications, status and experience should be challenged because by so doing they are confining schools when they should be liberating them.

- Fourthly, we should always be looking to question and challenge the status quo and allow all members of the organisation the time, space and wherewithal to review current practice and explore ways of improving it. We know that a complacent school is a coasting, underachieving one but it is deceptively easy to convince yourself that all is right with the world when people are not encouraged to look beneath the surface and find out what is really working and what is not. Note that external inspections are not guaranteed to arrive at the right judgements!

- Finally, schools have a vitally important role to play in the communities in which they operate, whether that is local, regional, national or international and they fail in a crucially important aspect of their work if they do not do everything they can to communicate with the wide range of stakeholders that they engage with. Only by doing this will they enable their students to become socially articulate and globally aware.

Conclusion

Of course we are in no doubt that every school leader will have his or her list of what sits at the heart of a really good school and we hope there will be a degree of empathy and support for the conclusions we have arrived at. The important thing to bear in mind is, however, that we probably all need to make a list of what we really believe in and then regularly and rigorously question and challenge it. Only by so doing will we avoid the trap of becoming 'all-knowing' and complacent.

It is highly unlikely that any school leader would ever think that he or she knows without question what makes for the highest quality teaching and learning and what constitutes the best and most effective school leadership. One of the real joys of teaching and of headship in particular is that you are always learning, always refining your skills and ideas secure in the knowledge that you will never completely resolve what it is that engages young minds and encourages them to go out and learn things. School leaders are well aware how demanding and ever-changing their roles and responsibilities are and how hard they will have to work to make an impact. But what an endlessly fascinating and exhilarating challenge to take on!

References

Begley, P. (2010), 'Leading with moral purpose; the place of ethics,' in T. Bush, L. Bell, L and D. Middlewood (eds), *The Principles of Educational Leadership and Management*. London: Sage.

Bell, L. and Bush, T. (2002), 'The policy context,' in T. Bush, L. Bell (eds), *The Principles and Practice of Educational Management*. London: Sage.

Bennis, W. and Nanus, B. (1985), *Leaders*. New York: McGraw Hill.

Bolman, T. and Deal, T. (1997), *Reframing Organisations: Artistry, Choice and Leadership*. San Francisco, Routledge Falmer.

Bush, T. (1996), *Theories of Educational Management* (second edition). London: Sage. (2008), *Leadership and Management Development in Eucation*. London: Sage.

Bush, T. and Middlewood, D. (2013), *Leading and Managing People in Education* (third edition). London: Sage.

Bush, T. and Odura, G. (2006), 'New principals in Africa: preparation, induction and practice' in the *South African Journal of Education*, 31 (1), 31-43.

Bush, T., Bell, L. and Middlewood, D. (2010), 'New directions in educational leadership,' in T. Bush, L. Bell and D. Middlewood (eds).

Canter L. and Canter M. (1992), *Assertive Discipline: Positive Behaviour Management for Today's Classroom*. Indiana: Solution Tree Press.

Collins, J. and Porras, J. (1991), *Organisational Vision and Visionary Organisation*. Stanford, Stanford University.

Covey, S. (1992), *The Seven Habits of Highly Effective People*. London: Simon and Schuster.

Crawford, M. (2003), 'Inventive management and wise leadership,' in N. Bennett, M. Crawford and M. Cartwright (eds), *Effective Educational Leadership*. London: Paul Chapman Publishing.

Cuban, L. (1988), *The Managerial Imperative and the Practice of Leadership*. New York: State University of New York Press.

Dimmock, C. and Donoghue, T. (1997), *Innovative School Principals and Restructuring*. London: Routledge.

Fayol, H. (1916), *General and Industrial Administration*. London: Pitman.

Fink, D. (2005), *Leadership for Mortals*. London: Paul Chapman Publishing.

Fullan, M. (1992), *Successful School Improvement*. Buckingham: Open University Press.

—(1998), 'Leadership for the twenty-first century: breaking the bonds of dependency'. *Educational Leadership*, 55 (7): 6-10.

Goleman, D. (1996), *Emotional Intelligence*. London: Bloomsbury.

Grint, K. (2003), 'The arts of leadership,' in N. Bennett, M. Crawford and M. Cartwright (eds), op. cit.

Gronn, P. (2003), *The New Work of Educational Leaders: Changing Leadership Practice in an Era of School Reform*. London: Paul Chapman.

Gronn, P. and Ribbins, P. (1996), 'Leaders in context'. *Education Administration Quarterly*, Vol 32, no 3, 452-473.

Harris, A. (2005), 'Foreword' in D. Fink, op. cit.

Heath, C. and Heath, D. (2010), *Switch: How to Change Things when Change is Hard*. Broadway books, New York: Random House

Hoyle, E. and Wallace, M. (2005), *Educational Leadership: Ambiguity, Professional and Managerialism*. London: Sage.

Kanter, R., Stein, B. and Jick, T. (1992), *The Challenge of Organisational Change: How Companies Experience It and Leaders Guide It*. NY: Simon and Schuster.

Litwaski, R. (2002), 'Taking a third headship'. *Headship Matters*, No. 19, London: Optimus.

Middlewood, D. (1997), 'Managing recruitment and selection,' in D. Middlewood and T. Bush (eds), *Managing People in Education*. London: Paul Chapman Publishing.

—(1998), 'Strategic management in education: an overview,' in D. Middlewood and J. Lumby (eds), *Strategic Management in Schools and Colleges*. London: Paul Chapman Publishing.

—(2010), 'Managing people and performance,' in T. Bush, L. Bell and D. Middlewood, (eds).

Middlewood, D., Parker, R. and Beere, J. (2005), *Creating a Learning School*. London: Paul Chapman Publishing.

Parker, R. (1997), 'The role of school leaders in monitoring and evaluating'. MBA dissertation (unpublished). Leicester: University of Leicester.

—(2002), 'Passion and intuition: the impact of life history on leadership'. Practitioner Enquiry Report. Nottingham: National College for School Leadership

Sergiovanni, T. (1991), *The Principalship: a Reflective Practice Perspective*. Boston, Allyn and Bacon.

Starratt, R. (1996), *Transforming Educational Administration: Meaning, Community and Excellence*. New York: McGraw Hill.

Stoll, L. and Fink, D. (1996). *Changing Our Schools: Linking School Effectiveness and School Improvement*. Buckingham: Open University Press.

Torrington, D. and Weightman, J. (1989), *The Reality of School Management*. Oxford: Blackwell.

Tyler, B. (2000), 'Preparing for retirement: goodbye Mr Chips' *Headship Matters*, Vol 1, No 5, London: Optimus.

Watson, L. (2003), 'Heads of schools: twenty three European perspectives. Sheffield: European Forum on Educational Administration.

West-Burnham, J. (1992), 'Management in educational organisations,' in T. Bush and J. West-Burnham (eds), *The Principles of Educational Management*. Harlow: Longman.

—(2002), 'Leadership and spirituality'. Seminar for Leading Edge. Nottingham: National College for School Leadership.

Woods, R. (2002), 'Enchanted headteachers: sustainability in primary school Headship'. Practitioner Enquiry Report. Nottingham: National College for School Leadership.

Yukl, G. (2002), *Leadership in Organisations* (fifth edition). New Jersey: Prentice-Hall.

Index